The RHYTHM of PRAYER

a forty day experience

mark a. moore

D0168751

wesleyan
publishing
house

Indianapolis, Indiana

Copyright © 2006 by Wesleyan Publishing House
Published by Wesleyan Publishing House
Indianapolis, Indiana 46250
Printed in the United States of America

ISBN-13: 978-0-89827-345-8
ISBN-10: 0-89827-345-5

All Scripture quotations, unless otherwise marked, are taken from *The Holy Bible, King James Version*.

Scripture quotations marked (*NIV*) are taken from the *Holy Bible, New International Version*®. *NIV*®. Copyright ©1973, 1978, 1984 by International Bible Society. Used by permission of Zondervan. All rights reserved.

Scripture quotations marked (The Message) are taken from *THE MESSAGE*. Copyright © by Eugene H. Peterson 1993, 1994, 1995, 1996, 2000, 2001, 2002. Used by permission of NavPress Publishing Group.

Scripture quotations marked (*NCV*) are taken from the *The Holy Bible, New Century Version*®, copyright © 2005 by Thomas Nelson, Inc. Used by permission.

Scripture quotations marked (*NLT*) are taken from the *Holy Bible, New Living Translation,* copyright © 1996. Used by permission of Tyndale House Publishers, Inc., Wheaton, IL 60189 USA. All rights reserved.

To my wife, Kelli, whose beauty brightens my life,
And to our son, Dylan

ACKNOWLEDGEMENTS

Several people played integral parts in the development of this project and deserve recognition here. Don Cady and Larry Wilson, along with the rest of the staff at Wesleyan Publishing House, made a new author feel welcomed and at ease. John Coe, Steve Porter, and the Institute for Spiritual Formation at Talbot provided a wonderful environment for learning and growth, from which the desire for this project emerged. The Reverend H. Ivor Kraft, Mary Brown, and Stephen Silke greatly supported my research and writing with warm conversation and honest friendship. And, of course, my family and friends—life is simply better because of you.

I f you had chanced to walk along Delancy Street on the Lower East Side during the summer of 1959, you might have heard the faint sounds of a tenor saxophone echoing off the massive steel girders of the Williamsburg Bridge, filling Manhattan's early morning air with gentle rhythm. The man behind the melodies was burgeoning jazz legend Sonny Rollins. By the age of nineteen, this self-taught virtuoso had collaborated with some of jazz's most innovative performers: Miles Davis, Theolonius Monk, Bud Powell, and Charlie "Bird" Parker. With the release of his masterpiece album, *Saxophone Collosus,* in 1956, Rollins, or "Newk" as he was known by friends, established himself as one of the most talented musicians of his time.

On the Williamsburg Bridge, though, Newk wasn't working on a concert set or arrangements for a new recording. He was withdrawing from the jazz scene altogether, taking an extended Sabbath at the height of his career to remaster the basics of jazz composition. Dissatisfied with the music business and the fame, Rollins felt that his ability to improvise on traditional jazz melodies had weakened because he had strayed too far from the foundational elements of his art—disciplines he insisted on maintaining even if it cost him his career. This hunger to create pure music struck Rollins a few years prior, during a concert at the Village Vanguard—an electric performance that produced, by many accounts, some of the most innovative improvisational recordings in jazz history. Yet he knew there was more.

Rollins understood that music has a basic structure, a foundation of scales and rhythms upon which all melodies are built. True improvisation has to bridge off of this foundation. Ignorance of it does not lead to innovation; it leads to shallow art. Offbeats and dissonant chords make sense only when intentionally placed within a structure of downbeat rhythms and consonant chords. To improvise only on previous improvisations, stifles creativity and transposes art into meaningless expressions. Improvisational jazz would sound no different than children banging on pots and pans were it not for the boundaries of rhythm and scale. Only skilled musicians, those who have studied the parameters of musicology, can improvise, bending the rules intentionally to speak to their audience. So when Sonny Rollins inserted a chord he knew did not fit, it was because he wanted his listeners to feel the tension; he created dissonance not for its own sake, but to be in contrast with harmony. Improvisation finds its power in intentionality.

So in 1959, Rollins returned to the roots of not only jazz composition but also basic music theory, using Nicolas Slonimsky's *Thesaurus of Scales and Melodic Patterns* as a guide. It was these melodic scales that a few lucky New Yorkers heard while making their morning commute during those stifling summer months.

Prayer is a mirror of music. It, too, has a basic structure, a foundation of theology and intentionality. Throughout history, Christians have developed the practice of prayer upon this base—a practice infused with Scripture, guided by the Spirit, and built upon basic elements. More recently, and rightly so, improvisational prayer has become common; yet it has brought with it the same weakness that Sonny Rollins detected in his music—the weakness that comes from straying too far from the basic structures of the form.

In his collection *Essays in Applied Christianity*, Reinhold Niebuhr spoke to the "weakness of common worship" as it related to American Protestantism and Evangelicalism. Niebuhr applauded the positives of Evangelicalism—its desire to touch hearts and souls with the Word of God and free worship—but he wondered if by 1950 the movement had already passed its prime. Just as Rollins explored the fundamental elements of music on the Bridge, Niebuhr encouraged evangelicals to create a new liturgy, one that might provide a meaningful foundation for their honest expressions of worship.

The evangelical, free-form worship movement that occurred in America early in the twentieth century was greatly needed. But now many of us seem to be improvising on that earlier improvisation. The result is a practice of prayer that has strayed too far from its roots. Our prayers are often self-serving because they lack a proper theology, and they are unintentional due to our own laziness.

The use of a prayer liturgy offers a return to the basic elements that make for a meaningful prayer life. Liturgy provides a structure, an intentionality—a rhythm—which we need in order to have a deep and meaningful experience in prayer. By using a prayer liturgy, improvisation is not replaced; it is grounded. Freedom is not constrained; it is focused.

THE BENEFIT OF A DAILY PRAYER LITURGY

A prayer liturgy is a guide for structuring a meaningful prayer experience. It places Scripture readings, written prayers, and times of contemplation into a set structure. For many, excessive freedom and a lack of structure have led to the absence of prayer, save for a few quick head bows before meals. It is not that the use of liturgy alone has the power to form our spirit but rather that the consistency provided by the liturgy acts as a catalyst in opening our souls in a daily rhythm before God and his Word. This rhythm escorts body and soul to a place where it is possible to experience a deep, consuming conversation with Almighty God.

A daily prayer liturgy provides consistency because it has rhythm, which is always intentional. Rhythm has a resolute timing that both draws us back and moves us forward. Not one prayer, Scripture reading, or intercession is placed in the liturgy by accident. Each word is carefully selected to open the soul to the Lord in contemplation and praise. A common problem with free-form worship is that it fails to intentionally direct the heart to God. An unintentional prayer life exhibits the same weakness.

Many Christians wonder how to gain consistency in their devotional life. Some start and restart devotional practices many times, reading the same few passages and praying more or less the same prayers over and over again. A daily prayer liturgy is directive; it leads us. It takes the guesswork out of what to do on any given day, providing a reliable starting point for prayer and Bible meditation. Rather than thumbing through the Bible each day, usually arriving at the Gospel of John or Psalm 23, we are gently guided into a contemplative moment based on a thoughtful offering of Scripture and prayer.

The muse and source of our creativity in prayer is the Holy Spirit. The Spirit leads us on the path of daily prayer, encouraging us, and pointing out areas where we need to pause and spend extended time in meditation. The Spirit fills our hearts with God's heart so that our prayers reflect his will. Currently, there is a great emphasis on maintaining personal freedom in prayer. In our enthusiasm to explore our own styles, though, we have forgotten that there is freedom within the lines. The creation of meaningful music, poetry, and visual arts demands innovation, yet each discipline has basic rules—lines that only experienced artists can cross without compromising the form.

Liturgical daily prayer is not a panacea for all devotional ills. It is a form, and like any form, it can grow cold and void of passion. Yet when the uncritical application of freedom has produced a passionless prayer life, a daily prayer liturgy can provide the impetus needed to reestablish the rhythm of prayer for which the heart longs.

THE METHOD OF THIS LITURGY

Daily liturgical prayer is a spiritual practice that has developed since the earliest days of the Church. As a young believer, I was introduced to this discipline by a journal article on praying the daily office—a regimen of praying at specific hours throughout the day. The article came at the right time in my life. I was hungry for a consistent devotional experience. I picked up a copy of *The Book of Common Prayer* but felt confused by the structure of the book, which divides the various elements of the liturgy into different sections throughout the work. I needed to see each element of the liturgy placed in sequence to truly appreciate the beauty of this form. That has been my desire in compiling this liturgy: to create an easy-to-follow introduction to the rhythm of daily prayer.

Before we proceed with the liturgy itself, let's walk through the elements included in this format. It may be helpful to think of each day as a unique song, with a unique melody and meter. Some days, the beat will be fast, the melody racing. On others, the cadence sporadic, the melody dissonant. Each one, however, will be built from the same elements—an intentional foundation—that will form the day's experience.

RUBRICS

In any prayer book, the rubrics are the basic directions for the liturgy—the fine print between each section. Traditional prayer books are used in public services and contain different elements separated by multiple pages. The rubrics for those prayer books serve as a conductor for the order of service, prescribing which hymn to sing or antiphon to use on a given holy day. Because this liturgy is designed for personal use, I have reinvented the rubrics as subtle worship prompts. They will guide you through each day's prayers and Scripture selections.

OPENING SENTENCE

Seven different sentences are used to open this liturgy, all adapted from various psalms. They are repeated in a seven-day cycle. Internalize these calls to worship, and allow them to direct your thoughts toward God.

After each opening sentence, the liturgy continues with an adaptation of the *Gloria Patri*—a common refrain from the early Church, which offers praise to the triune, unchanging nature of God.

INVITATORY PSALM

After the opening sentence and Gloria Patri, a psalm is read as an invitation to praise. These invitatory psalms also are repeated on a seven-day cycle. The phrases in italics are antiphons, which were used in corporate prayer services as responses that reinforce the message of the psalm. Take your time here, and say each word with purpose.

PRAYER OF CONFESSION

After the invitation of worship has been accepted, time is allowed to prepare your heart and mind through confession. You will notice that the voice is plural—a reminder that you are not alone. We are each a part of one body. Allow the Holy Spirit to indicate the amount of time to be spent in this section each day. On some days it will be brief. On others, you may spend your entire devotional time on this element.

THE PSALTER

Following this moment of honest reflection, you will read another psalm. The psalms chosen for this forty-day liturgy come from Book I (Psalms 1–41) and Book IV (Psalms 90–106), which prompt us to worship God for the mighty works he has done. The Latin titles for each psalm, which are simply the first few words of the psalm, are also included here to give a sense of the long history of praying the psalms.

READING FROM SACRED SCRIPTURE

Next you will read a longer portion of Scripture. This liturgy uses selections from Paul's letters to the Ephesians and Romans, as well as large portions from the book of Isaiah. Remember that Scripture is one of the elements that makes prayer a dialogue. This is God's part of the conversation. Listen with an open heart.

INTERCESSION

Now comes the time for you to express your own needs in your own way. Fill this time with prayers of petition or praise. Following this time of personal prayer, a written intercession is read. As with the opening sentences and invitatory psalms, seven intercessions have been chosen and are repeated. The first two of these intercessions are suffrages, brief prayers that have been passed down in liturgies throughout Church history. The rest are adaptations I have created using Scriptures ranging from Psalm 30 to the Beatitudes.

THE LORD'S PRAYER

When Christ's disciples were seeking a structure for the spiritual life, they inquired of Jesus, "Lord, teach us to pray, just as John taught his disciples" (Luke 11:1 NLT). Jesus didn't reply with a long sermon on the nature of prayer, nor did he direct the disciples to do whatever they felt like doing. His lesson on prayer was a prayer.

He said, "This is how you should pray:

Father, may your name be honored.
May your Kingdom come soon.
Give us our food day by day.
And forgive our sins—
just as we forgive those who have sinned against us.
And don't let us yield to temptation" (Luke 11:2–4 NLT).

Jesus gave us a form-prayer, not to teach us what to say in prayer, but to exemplify the proper spirit to have in prayer. The Lord's Prayer is included in this liturgy as a continual reminder against making selfish prayers. First and foremost, Jesus praised God. He asked only for sustenance, forgiveness, and the will of the Father. We do well to do the same.

SILENCE

Between the Lord's Prayer and the concluding prayer, a moment of silent meditation is directed by the rubrics. Again, the amount of time spent here will fluctuate by day; life happens and schedules constrain.

CONCLUDING PRAYER

A Scripture-infused written prayer concludes each day's liturgy. Six original prayers are used in this liturgy, each one repeated for seven consecutive days (with the exception of the last of the six prayers, which is repeated for only five consecutive days). They bring closure to each day's liturgy and form a benediction upon the day.

So pause and take a deep breath. Listen for the downbeat, and pray in step with God's rhythm.

Quiet your heart before the LORD, then proceed as you feel ready.

LORD, open our lips,
>And our mouths shall proclaim your praise.

Glory to the Father, and to the Son, and to the Holy Spirit. As it was in the beginning, is now, and will be forever: from unending to unending. Amen.

For the mighty works of God, lift your praises.

PSALM 100
Jubilate Deo

Make a joyful noise unto the LORD, all ye lands.
Serve the LORD with gladness:
>come before his presence with singing.
Be joyful in the LORD, all you lands.
Know ye that the LORD he is God:
>it is he that hath made us, and not we ourselves;
>we are his people, and the sheep of his pasture.
Be joyful in the LORD, all you lands.
Enter into his gates with thanksgiving,
>and into his courts with praise:
>be thankful unto him, and bless his name.
Be joyful in the LORD, all you lands.
For the LORD is good; his mercy is everlasting;
>and his truth endureth to all generations.
His love and mercy endure forever.

Let us kneel and ask God to cleanse us from all unrighteousness.

PRAYER OF CONFESSION

Most holy and gracious God, we confess to you that we don't always get it right. We don't always love as you have called us to love. We don't often enough answer your invitation to serve. We don't continually seek the lost. But Father, you get it right with us every time. Accept our humble confession, and sanctify us by the power and beauty of your Word, that we may live in the light of your goodness, serve with the warmth of your gentleness, and love with the passion of your grace. Forever and ever, let it be so.

Pause for a moment to reflect on your repentance.

Then join with the psalmist's heart, giving praise and adoration.

PSALM 1
Beatus Vir Qui non Abiit

Blessed is the man
>that walketh not in the counsel of the ungodly,
>nor standeth in the way of sinners,
>nor sitteth in the seat of the scornful.
But his delight is in the law of the LORD;
>and in his law doth he meditate day and night.
And he shall be like a tree planted by the rivers of water,
>that bringeth forth his fruit in his season;
>his leaf also shall not wither;
>and whatsoever he doeth shall prosper.
The ungodly are not so:
>but are like the chaff
>which the wind driveth away.
Therefore the ungodly shall not stand in the judgment,
>nor sinners in the congregation of the righteous.
For the LORD knoweth the way of the righteous:
>but the way of the ungodly shall perish.

Open your ears to hear the Word of the Lord.

A READING FROM SACRED SCRIPTURE
Ephesians 1:3–14 (The Message)

How blessed is God! And what a blessing he is! He's the Father of our Master, Jesus Christ, and takes us to the high places of blessing in him. Long before he laid down earth's foundations, he had us in mind, had settled on us as the focus of his love, to be made whole and holy by his love. Long, long ago he decided to adopt us into his family through Jesus Christ. (What pleasure he took in planning this!) He wanted us to enter into the celebration of his lavish gift-giving by the hand of his beloved Son.

Because of the sacrifice of the Messiah, his blood poured out on the altar of the Cross, we're a free people—free of penalties and punishments chalked up by all our misdeeds. And not just barely free, either. Abundantly free! He thought of everything, provided for everything we could possibly need, letting us in on the plans he took such delight in making. He set it all out before us in Christ, a long-range plan in which everything would be brought together and summed up in him, everything in deepest heaven, everything on planet earth.

It's in Christ that we find out who we are and what we are living for. Long before we first heard of Christ and got our hopes up, he had his eye on us, had designs on us for glorious living, part of the overall purpose he is working out in everything and everyone.

It's in Christ that you, once you heard the truth and believed it (this Message of your salvation), found yourselves home free— signed, sealed, and delivered by the Holy Spirit. This signet from God is the first installment on what's coming, a reminder that we'll get everything God has planned for us, a praising and glorious life.

The Word of the Lord.
Thanks be to God.

Pray now for your own needs and for the needs of others.

Allot ample time to freely express your prayers.

INTERCESSION

Save your people, Lord, and bless your inheritance;
Govern and uphold them, now and always.
Day by day we bless you;
We praise your name forever.
Lord, keep us from all sin today;
Have mercy on us, Lord, have mercy.
Lord, show us your love and mercy;
For we put our trust in you.
In you, Lord, is our hope;
And we shall never hope in vain.

The disciples inquired, "Lord, teach us to pray." We join with his reply.

THE LORD'S PRAYER

Our Father, who art in heaven, hallowed be thy name. Thy Kingdom come, thy will be done, on earth as it is in heaven. Give us this day our daily bread. And forgive us our trespasses, as we forgive those who trespass against us. And lead us not into temptation, but deliver us from evil.

Spend a few moments in silence, meditating on the Lord.

CONCLUDING PRAYER

Everlasting God, you have been faithful in your promise to never leave us nor forsake us. May you set us apart this day to be holy, to be wholly yours, so that with each movement of the hours, our hearts will be drawn to you in loving prayer and honest devotion. In the blessed name of your Son, our Lord Jesus Christ, and in the fellowship of the Holy Spirit, amen.

Quiet your heart before the Lord, then proceed as you feel ready.

May the words of our mouths
    And the meditations of our hearts
Be pleasing in your sight,
    O LORD, our Rock and our Redeemer.

Glory to the Father, and to the Son, and to the Holy Spirit. As it was in the beginning, is now, and will be forever: from unending to unending. Amen.

For the mighty works of God, lift your praises.

PSALM 147:1–9
Laudate Domine

Praise ye the LORD:
    for it is good to sing praises unto our God;
    for it is pleasant; and praise is comely.
It is good to praise the LORD.
The LORD doth build up Jerusalem:
    he gathereth together the outcasts of Israel.
He healeth the broken in heart,
    and bindeth up their wounds.
The LORD is worthy of praise.
He telleth the number of the stars;
    he calleth them all by their names.
Great is our Lord, and of great power:
    his understanding is infinite.

The LORD lifteth up the meek:
>he casteth the wicked down to the ground.

Our God is great and mighty.

Sing unto the LORD with thanksgiving;
>sing praise upon the harp unto our God:

Who covereth the heaven with clouds,
>who prepareth rain for the earth,
>who maketh grass to grow upon the mountains.

He giveth to the beast his food,
>and to the young ravens which cry.

Sing to the LORD who provides.

Let us kneel and ask God to cleanse us from all unrighteousness.

PRAYER OF CONFESSION

Most holy and gracious God, we confess to you that we don't always get it right. We don't always love as you have called us to love. We don't often enough answer your invitation to serve. We don't continually seek the lost. But Father, you get it right with us every time. Accept our humble confession, and sanctify us by the power and beauty of your Word, that we may live in the light of your goodness, serve with the warmth of your gentleness, and love with the passion of your grace. Forever and ever, let it be so.

Pause for a moment to reflect on your repentance.

Then join with the psalmist's heart, giving praise and adoration.

PSALM 3:1–6
Domine, Quid Multiplicati?

LORD, how are they increased that trouble me!
>many are they that rise up against me.

Many there be which say of my soul,
>There is no help for him in God.
>Selah.

But thou, O LORD, art a shield for me;

my glory, and the lifter up of mine head.
I cried unto the LORD with my voice,
 and he heard me out of his holy hill.
 Selah.
I laid me down and slept;
 I awaked; for the LORD sustained me.
I will not be afraid of ten thousands of people,
 that have set themselves against me round about.

Open your ears to hear the Word of the Lord.

A READING FROM SACRED SCRIPTURE
Isaiah 2:12–18 (NCV)

The LORD All-Powerful has a certain day planned
 when he will punish the proud and those who brag,
 and they will no longer be important.
He will bring down the tall cedar trees from Lebanon
 and the great oak trees of Bashan,
all the tall mountains
 and the high hills,
every tall tower
 and every high, strong wall,
all the trading ships
 and the beautiful ships.
At that time proud people will be made humble,
 and they will bow low with shame.
At that time only the LORD will be praised,
 but all the idols will be gone.

The Word of the Lord.
Thanks be to God.

Pray now for your own needs and for the needs of others.

Allot ample time to freely express your prayers.

INTERCESSION

We will exalt your name, O Lord,
For you have heard our cries,
And you have healed us.
The Lord has lifted us up from the depths.
We will sing praises to you our Lord,
For your anger is fleeting,
But your favor lasts forever.
The Lord has lifted us up from the depths.
Our hearts cannot stay silent,
Forever we will give you thanks.
The Lord has lifted us up from the depths.

The disciples inquired, "Lord, teach us to pray." We join with his reply.

THE LORD'S PRAYER

Our Father, who art in heaven, hallowed be thy name. Thy Kingdom come, thy will be done, on earth as it is in heaven. Give us this day our daily bread. And forgive us our trespasses, as we forgive those who trespass against us. And lead us not into temptation, but deliver us from evil.

Spend a few moments in silence, meditating on the Lord.

CONCLUDING PRAYER

Everlasting God, you have been faithful in your promise to never leave us nor forsake us. May you set us apart this day to be holy, to be wholly yours, so that with each movement of the hours, our hearts will be drawn to you in loving prayer and honest devotion. In the blessed name of your Son, our Lord Jesus Christ, and in the fellowship of the Holy Spirit, amen.

2/8/08

Quiet your heart before the Lord, then proceed as you feel ready.

Teach us your way, O LORD,
    And we will walk in your truth.
Give us undivided hearts,
    That we may fear your name.

Glory to the Father, and to the Son, and to the Holy Spirit. As it was in the beginning, is now, and will be forever: from unending to unending. Amen.

For the mighty works of God, lift your praises.

PSALM 149:1–4
Cantate Domino

Praise ye the LORD.
    Sing unto the LORD a new song,
    and his praise in the congregation of saints.
Sing to the LORD a new song.
Let Israel rejoice in him that made him:
    let the children of Zion be joyful in their King.
Let them praise his name in the dance:
    let them sing praises unto him with the timbrel and harp.
Make music for the LORD our God.
For the LORD taketh pleasure in his people:
    he will beautify the meek with salvation.
For the LORD saves us.

Let us kneel and ask God to cleanse us from all unrighteousness.

PRAYER OF CONFESSION

Most holy and gracious God, we confess to you that we don't always get it right. We don't always love as you have called us to love. We don't often enough answer your invitation to serve. We don't continually seek the lost. But Father, you get it right with us every time. Accept our humble confession, and sanctify us by the power and beauty of your Word, that we may live in the light of your goodness, serve with the warmth of your gentleness, and love with the passion of your grace. Forever and ever, let it be so.

Pause for a moment to reflect on your repentance.

Then join with the psalmist's heart, giving praise and adoration.

PSALM 5:1–8
Verba Mea Auribus

Give ear to my words, O LORD,
    consider my meditation.
Hearken unto the voice of my cry,
    my King, and my God:
    for unto thee will I pray.
My voice shalt thou hear in the morning, O LORD;
    in the morning will I direct my prayer unto thee,
    and will look up.
For thou art not a God that hath pleasure in wickedness:
    neither shall evil dwell with thee.
The foolish shall not stand in thy sight:
    thou hatest all workers of iniquity.
Thou shalt destroy them that speak leasing:
    the LORD will abhor
    the bloody and deceitful man.
But as for me, I will come into thy house
    in the multitude of thy mercy:
    and in thy fear will I worship

toward thy holy temple.
Lead me, O LORD, in thy righteousness
    because of mine enemies;
    make thy way straight before my face.

Open your ears to hear the Word of the Lord.

A READING FROM SACRED SCRIPTURE
Isaiah 5:1–7 (NCV)

Now I will sing for my friend a song about his vineyard.
My friend had a vineyard
    on a hill with very rich soil.
He dug and cleared the field of stones
    and planted the best grapevines there.
He built a tower in the middle of it
    and cut out a winepress as well.
He hoped good grapes would grow there,
    but only bad ones grew.
My friend says, "You people living in Jerusalem,
    and you people of Judah,
    judge between me and my vineyard.
What more could I have done for my vineyard
    than I have already done?
Although I expected good grapes to grow,
    why were there only bad ones?
Now I will tell you
    what I will do to my vineyard:
I will remove the hedge,
    and it will be burned.
I will break down the stone wall,
    and it will be walked on.
I will ruin my field.
    It will not be trimmed or hoed,
    and weeds and thorns will grow there.
I will command the clouds
    not to rain on it."

The vineyard belonging to the LORD All-Powerful
 is the nation of Israel;
the garden that he loves
 is the people of Judah.
He looked for justice, but there was only killing.
 He hoped for right living, but there were only cries of pain.

The Word of the Lord.
Thanks be to God.

Pray now for your own needs and for the needs of others.

Allot ample time to freely express your prayers.

INTERCESSION

The earth is yours and everything in it;
 King of Glory, hear our prayers.
You founded it upon the sea, upon the waters;
 King of Glory, hear our prayers.
You clean our hands from the dirt of our sin;
 King of Glory, hear our prayers.
You lead us up the mountain, your holy hill;
 King of Glory, hear our prayers.
Who is this King of Glory?
 The Lord Almighty—he will hear our prayers.

The disciples inquired, "Lord, teach us to pray." We join with his reply.

THE LORD'S PRAYER

Our Father, who art in heaven, hallowed be thy name. Thy Kingdom come, thy will be done, on earth as it is in heaven. Give us this day our daily bread. And forgive us our trespasses, as we forgive those who trespass against us. And lead us not into temptation, but deliver us from evil.

Spend a few moments in silence, meditating on the Lord.

CONCLUDING PRAYER

Everlasting God, you have been faithful in your promise to never leave us nor forsake us. May you set us apart this day to be holy, to be wholly yours, so that with each movement of the hours, our hearts will be drawn to you in loving prayer and honest devotion. In the blessed name of your Son, our Lord Jesus Christ, and in the fellowship of the Holy Spirit, amen.

2/9/08

DAY FOUR

Quiet your heart before the Lord, then proceed as you feel ready.

Give thanks to the LORD,
    And call upon his name.
Make known among the nations
    The great works he has done.

Glory to the Father, and to the Son, and to the Holy Spirit. As it was in the beginning, is now, and will be forever: from unending to unending. Amen.

For the mighty works of God, lift your praises.

PSALM 95:1–7
Venite Exultemus

O come, let us sing unto the LORD:
    let us make a joyful noise to the rock of our salvation.

Let us come before his presence with thanksgiving,
  and make a joyful noise unto him with psalms.
Let us shout to the Rock.
For the LORD is a great God,
  and a great King above all gods.
In his hand are the deep places of the earth:
  the strength of the hills is his also.
The sea is his, and he made it:
  and his hands formed the dry land.
Let us worship our Lord, our Creator.
O come, let us worship and bow down:
  let us kneel before the LORD our maker.
For he is our God;
  and we are the people of his pasture,
  and the sheep of his hand.
For he is the Great Shepherd.

Let us kneel and ask God to cleanse us from all unrighteousness.

PRAYER OF CONFESSION

Most holy and gracious God, we confess to you that we don't always get it right. We don't always love as you have called us to love. We don't often enough answer your invitation to serve. We don't continually seek the lost. But Father, you get it right with us every time. Accept our humble confession, and sanctify us by the power and beauty of your Word, that we may live in the light of your goodness, serve with the warmth of your gentleness, and love with the passion of your grace. Forever and ever, let it be so.

Pause for a moment to reflect on your repentance.

Then join with the psalmist's heart, giving praise and adoration.

PSALM 8

Domine, Dominus Noster

O LORD, our Lord,
>   how excellent is thy name in all the earth!
>   who hast set thy glory above the heavens.

Out of the mouth of babes and sucklings
>   hast thou ordained strength
>   because of thine enemies,
>   that thou mightest still the enemy and the avenger.

When I consider thy heavens,
>   the work of thy fingers,
>   the moon and the stars,
>   which thou hast ordained;

What is man, that thou art mindful of him?
>   and the son of man, that thou visitest him?

For thou hast made him a little lower than the angels,
>   and hast crowned him with glory and honour.

Thou madest him to have dominion over the works of thy hands;
>   thou hast put all things under his feet:

All sheep and oxen, yea,
>   and the beasts of the field;

The fowl of the air,
>   and the fish of the sea,
>   and whatsoever passeth through the paths of the seas.

O LORD our Lord,
>   how excellent is thy name in all the earth!

Open your ears to hear the Word of the Lord.

A READING FROM SACRED SCRIPTURE
Romans 1:8–20 (NIV)

First, I thank my God through Jesus Christ for all of you, because your faith is being reported all over the world. God, whom I serve with my whole heart in preaching the gospel of his Son, is my witness how constantly I remember you in my prayers at all times; and I pray that now at last by God's will the way may be opened for me to come to you.

I long to see you so that I may impart to you some spiritual gift to make you strong—that is, that you and I may be mutually encouraged by each other's faith. I do not want you to be unaware, brothers, that I planned many times to come to you (but have been prevented from doing so until now) in order that I might have a harvest among you, just as I have had among the other Gentiles.

I am obligated both to Greeks and non-Greeks, both to the wise and the foolish. That is why I am so eager to preach the gospel also to you who are at Rome.

I am not ashamed of the gospel, because it is the power of God for the salvation of everyone who believes: first for the Jew, then for the Gentile. For in the gospel a righteousness from God is revealed, a righteousness that is by faith from first to last, just as it is written: "The righteous will live by faith."

The wrath of God is being revealed from heaven against all the godlessness and wickedness of men who suppress the truth by their wickedness, since what may be known about God is plain to them, because God has made it plain to them. For since the creation of the world God's invisible qualities—his eternal power and divine nature—have been clearly seen, being understood from what has been made, so that men are without excuse.

The Word of the Lord.
Thanks be to God.

Pray now for your own needs and for the needs of others.

Allot ample time to freely express your prayers.

INTERCESSION

Blessed are the poor in spirit,
> *For theirs is the kingdom of heaven.*
Blessed are those who mourn,
> *For they will be comforted.*
Blessed are the meek,

For they will inherit the earth.
Blessed are those who hunger for righteousness,
For they will be filled.
Blessed are the merciful,
For they will be shown mercy.
Blessed are the pure in heart,
For they will see God.
Blessed are the peacemakers,
For they will be called sons of God.

The disciples inquired, "Lord, teach us to pray." We join with his reply.

THE LORD'S PRAYER

Our Father, who art in heaven, hallowed be thy name. Thy Kingdom come, thy will be done, on earth as it is in heaven. Give us this day our daily bread. And forgive us our trespasses, as we forgive those who trespass against us. And lead us not into temptation, but deliver us from evil.

Spend a few moments in silence, meditating on the Lord.

CONCLUDING PRAYER

Everlasting God, you have been faithful in your promise to never leave us nor forsake us. May you set us apart this day to be holy, to be wholly yours, so that with each movement of the hours, our hearts will be drawn to you in loving prayer and honest devotion. In the blessed name of your Son, our Lord Jesus Christ, and in the fellowship of the Holy Spirit, amen.

Quiet your heart before the Lord, then proceed as you feel ready.

From the rising of the sun,
    The name of the LORD is to be praised.
To the place where it sets,
    The name of the LORD is to be praised.

Glory to the Father, and to the Son, and to the Holy Spirit. As it was in the beginning, is now, and will be forever: from unending to unending. Amen.

For the mighty works of God, lift your praises.

PSALM 146:1–8

Lauda, Anima Mea

Praise ye the LORD.
    Praise the LORD, O my soul.
While I live will I praise the LORD:
    I will sing praises unto my God while I have any being.
Praise the LORD, O my soul.
Put not your trust in princes,
    nor in the son of man, in whom there is no help.
His breath goeth forth, he returneth to his earth;
    in that very day his thoughts perish.
Praise the LORD, O my soul.
Happy is he that hath the God of Jacob for his help,
    whose hope is in the LORD his God:
Which made heaven, and earth,

the sea, and all that therein is:
    which keepeth truth for ever:
Praise the LORD, O my soul.
Which executeth judgment for the oppressed:
    which giveth food to the hungry.
The LORD looseth the prisoners:
The LORD openeth the eyes of the blind:
    the LORD raiseth them that are bowed down:
    the LORD loveth the righteous:
Praise the LORD, O my soul.

Let us kneel and ask God to cleanse us from all unrighteousness.

PRAYER OF CONFESSION

Most holy and gracious God, we confess to you that we don't always get it right. We don't always love as you have called us to love. We don't often enough answer your invitation to serve. We don't continually seek the lost. But Father, you get it right with us every time. Accept our humble confession, and sanctify us by the power and beauty of your Word, that we may live in the light of your goodness, serve with the warmth of your gentleness, and love with the passion of your grace. Forever and ever, let it be so.

Pause for a moment to reflect on your repentance.

Then join with the psalmist's heart, giving praise and adoration.

PSALM 9:1–10
Confitebor Tibi

I will praise thee, O LORD, with my whole heart;
    I will shew forth all thy marvellous works.
I will be glad and rejoice in thee:
    I will sing praise to thy name, O thou most High.
When mine enemies are turned back,
    they shall fall and perish at thy presence.
For thou hast maintained my right and my cause;

thou satest in the throne judging right.
Thou hast rebuked the heathen, thou hast destroyed the
        wicked,
    thou hast put out their name for ever and ever.
O thou enemy, destructions are come to a perpetual end:
    and thou hast destroyed cities;
    their memorial is perished with them.
But the LORD shall endure for ever:
    he hath prepared his throne for judgment.
And he shall judge the world in righteousness,
    he shall minister judgment to the people in uprightness.
The LORD also will be a refuge for the oppressed,
    a refuge in times of trouble.
And they that know thy name will put their trust in thee:
    for thou, LORD, hast not forsaken them that seek thee.

Open your ears to hear the Word of the Lord.

A READING FROM SACRED SCRIPTURE
Isaiah 6:1–8 (NCV)

In the year that King Uzziah died, I saw the Lord sitting on a very high throne. His long robe filled the Temple. Heavenly creatures of fire stood above him. Each creature had six wings: It used two wings to cover its face, two wings to cover its feet, and two wings for flying. Each creature was calling to the others:
    "Holy, holy, holy is the LORD All-Powerful.
    His glory fills the whole earth."
Their calling caused the frame around the door to shake, as the Temple filled with smoke.
    I said, "Oh, no! I will be destroyed. I am not pure, and I live among people who are not pure, but I have seen the King, the LORD All-Powerful."
    One of the heavenly creatures used a pair of tongs to take a hot coal from the altar. Then he flew to me with the hot coal in his hand. The creature touched my mouth with the hot coal and said, "Look, your guilt is taken away, because this hot coal has touched your

lips. Your sin is taken away."
Then I heard the Lord's voice, saying, "Whom can I send?
Who will go for us?"
So I said, "Here I am. Send me!"

The Word of the Lord.
Thanks be to God.

Pray now for your own needs and for the needs of others.

Allot ample time to freely express your prayers.

INTERCESSION

Cleanse me with hyssop, and I will be clean;
Wash me, and I will be whiter than snow.
Hide your face from my sins
And blot out all my iniquity.
Create in me a pure heart, O God,
And renew a steadfast spirit within me.
Do not cast me from your presence
Or take your Holy Spirit from me.
Restore to me the joy of your salvation
And grant me a willing spirit, to sustain me.

The disciples inquired, "Lord, teach us to pray." We join with his reply.

THE LORD'S PRAYER

Our Father, who art in heaven, hallowed be thy name. Thy Kingdom
come, thy will be done, on earth as it is in heaven. Give us this day
our daily bread. And forgive us our trespasses, as we forgive those
who trespass against us. And lead us not into temptation, but deliver
us from evil.

Spend a few moments in silence, meditating on the Lord.

CONCLUDING PRAYER

Everlasting God, you have been faithful in your promise to never leave us nor forsake us. May you set us apart this day to be holy, to be wholly yours, so that with each movement of the hours, our hearts will be drawn to you in loving prayer and honest devotion. In the blessed name of your Son, our Lord Jesus Christ, and in the fellowship of the Holy Spirit, amen.

DAY SIX

Quiet your heart before the Lord, then proceed as you feel ready.

Love the LORD,
    All you his saints.
Love the LORD your God,
    All you his faithful.

Glory to the Father, and to the Son, and to the Holy Spirit. As it was in the beginning, is now, and will be forever: from unending to unending. Amen.

For the mighty works of God, lift your praises.

PSALM 67
Deus Misereatur

God be merciful unto us, and bless us;
    and cause his face to shine upon us;

Selah.

That thy way may be known upon earth,
>   thy saving health among all nations.

O God, shine upon us.

Let the people praise thee, O God;
>   let all the people praise thee.

O let the nations be glad and sing for joy:
>   for thou shalt judge the people righteously,
>   and govern the nations upon earth.
>   Selah.

Let the people praise thee, O God;
>   let all the people praise thee.

O God, may we, your people, praise you.

Then shall the earth yield her increase;
>   and God, even our own God, shall bless us.

God shall bless us;
>   and all the ends of the earth shall fear him.

O God, may we, your people, praise you.

Let us kneel and ask God to cleanse us from all unrighteousness.

PRAYER OF CONFESSION

Most holy and gracious God, we confess to you that we don't always get it right. We don't always love as you have called us to love. We don't often enough answer your invitation to serve. We don't continually seek the lost. But Father, you get it right with us every time. Accept our humble confession, and sanctify us by the power and beauty of your Word, that we may live in the light of your goodness, serve with the warmth of your gentleness, and love with the passion of your grace. Forever and ever, let it be so.

Pause for a moment to reflect on your repentance.

Then join with the psalmist's heart, giving praise and adoration.

PSALM 11

In Domino Confido

In the LORD put I my trust:
>how say ye to my soul,
>Flee as a bird to your mountain?
For, lo, the wicked bend their bow,
>they make ready their arrow upon the string,
>that they may privily shoot
>at the upright in heart.
If the foundations be destroyed,
>what can the righteous do?
The LORD is in his holy temple,
>the LORD'S throne is in heaven:
>his eyes behold, his eyelids try, the children of men.
The LORD trieth the righteous:
>but the wicked and him that loveth violence
>his soul hateth.
Upon the wicked he shall rain snares,
>fire and brimstone,
>and an horrible tempest: this shall be the portion of their cup.
For the righteous LORD loveth righteousness;
>his countenance doth behold the upright.

Open your ears to hear the Word of the Lord.

A READING FROM SACRED SCRIPTURE
Romans 2:17–29 (NIV)

Now you, if you call yourself a Jew; if you rely on the law and brag about your relationship to God; if you know his will and approve of what is superior because you are instructed by the law; if you are convinced that you are a guide for the blind, a light for those who are in the dark, an instructor of the foolish, a teacher of infants, because you have in the law the embodiment of knowledge and truth—you, then, who teach others, do you not teach yourself? You who preach against stealing, do you steal? You who say that people should not commit adultery, do you commit adultery? You who abhor idols, do you rob temples? You who brag about the law, do you dishonor God by breaking the law? As it is written: "God's name is blasphemed among the Gentiles because of you."

Circumcision has value if you observe the law, but if you break the law, you have become as though you had not been circumcised. If those who are not circumcised keep the law's requirements, will they not be regarded as though they were circumcised? The one who is not circumcised physically and yet obeys the law will condemn you who, even though you have the written code and circumcision, are a lawbreaker.

A man is not a Jew if he is only one outwardly, nor is circumcision merely outward and physical. No, a man is a Jew if he is one inwardly; and circumcision is circumcision of the heart, by the Spirit, not by the written code. Such a man's praise is not from men, but from God.

The Word of the Lord.
Thanks be to God.

Pray now for your own needs and for the needs of others.

Allot ample time to freely express your prayers.

INTERCESSION

Show us your mercy, O Lord;
And grant us your salvation.
Clothe your ministers with righteousness;
Let your people sing with joy.
Give peace, O Lord, in all the world;
For only in you can we live in safety.
Lord, keep this nation under your care;
And guide us in the way of justice and truth.
Let your way be known upon earth;
Your saving health among all nations.
Let not the needy, O Lord, be forgotten;
Nor the hope of the poor be taken away.

Create in us clean hearts, O God;
  And sustain us with your Holy Spirit.

The disciples inquired, "Lord, teach us to pray." We join with his reply.

THE LORD'S PRAYER

Our Father, who art in heaven, hallowed be thy name. Thy Kingdom come, thy will be done, on earth as it is in heaven. Give us this day our daily bread. And forgive us our trespasses, as we forgive those who trespass against us. And lead us not into temptation, but deliver us from evil.

Spend a few moments in silence, meditating on the Lord.

CONCLUDING PRAYER

Everlasting God, you have been faithful in your promise to never leave us nor forsake us. May you set us apart this day to be holy, to be wholly yours, so that with each movement of the hours, our hearts will be drawn to you in loving prayer and honest devotion. In the blessed name of your Son, our Lord Jesus Christ, and in the fellowship of the Holy Spirit, amen.

Quiet your heart before the Lord, then proceed as you feel ready.

Ascribe to the LORD
　The glory due his name.
Worship the LORD
　In the splendor of his holiness.

Glory to the Father, and to the Son, and to the Holy Spirit. As it was in the beginning, is now, and will be forever: from unending to unending. Amen.

For the mighty works of God, lift your praises.

PSALM 148:1–12
Laudate Dominum

Praise ye the LORD.
　Praise ye the LORD from the heavens:
　praise him in the heights.
Praise ye him, all his angels:
　praise ye him, all his hosts.
Let us praise the LORD.
Praise ye him, sun and moon:
　praise him, all ye stars of light.
Praise him, ye heavens of heavens,
　and ye waters that be above the heavens.
Let them praise the name of the LORD:
　for he commanded, and they were created.
He hath also stablished them for ever and ever:
　he hath made a decree which shall not pass.

Let them praise the LORD.
Praise the LORD from the earth,
　ye dragons, and all deeps:
Fire, and hail; snow, and vapour;
　stormy wind fulfilling his word:
Mountains, and all hills;
　fruitful trees, and all cedars:
Beasts, and all cattle;
　creeping things, and flying fowl:
Kings of the earth, and all people;
　princes, and all judges of the earth:
Both young men, and maidens;
　old men, and children:
Let all voices praise the LORD.

Let us kneel and ask God to cleanse us from all unrighteousness.

PRAYER OF CONFESSION

Most holy and gracious God, we confess to you that we don't always get it right. We don't always love as you have called us to love. We don't often enough answer your invitation to serve. We don't continually seek the lost. But Father, you get it right with us every time. Accept our humble confession, and sanctify us by the power and beauty of your Word, that we may live in the light of your goodness, serve with the warmth of your gentleness, and love with the passion of your grace. Forever and ever, let it be so.

Pause for a moment to reflect on your repentance.

Then join with the psalmist's heart, giving praise and adoration.

PSALM 13
Usquequo, Domine?

How long wilt thou forget me, O LORD? for ever?
　how long wilt thou hide thy face from me?
How long shall I take counsel in my soul,

having sorrow in my heart daily?
how long shall mine enemy be exalted over me?
Consider and hear me, O LORD my God:
lighten mine eyes, lest I sleep the sleep of death;
Lest mine enemy say, I have prevailed against him;
and those that trouble me rejoice when I am moved.
But I have trusted in thy mercy;
my heart shall rejoice in thy salvation.
I will sing unto the LORD,
because he hath dealt bountifully with me.

Open your ears to hear the Word of the Lord.

A READING FROM SACRED SCRIPTURE
Isaiah 9:1–7 (NCV)

But suddenly there will be no more gloom for the land that suffered.
In the past God made the lands of Zebulun and Naphtali hang their
heads in shame, but in the future those lands will be made great. They
will stretch from the road along the Mediterranean Sea to the land
beyond the Jordan River and north to Galilee, the land of people who
are not Israelites.
Before those people lived in darkness,
but now they have seen a great light.
They lived in a dark land,
but a light has shined on them.
God, you have caused the nation to grow
and made the people happy.
And they have shown their happiness to you,
like the joy during harvest time,
like the joy of people
taking what they have won in war.
Like the time you defeated Midian,
you have taken away their heavy load
and the heavy pole from their backs
and the rod the enemy used to punish them.
Every boot that marched in battle

and every uniform stained with blood
has been thrown into the fire.
A child has been born to us;
    God has given a son to us.
    He will be responsible for leading the people.
His name will be Wonderful Counselor, Powerful God,
    Father Who Lives Forever, Prince of Peace.
Power and peace will be in his kingdom
    and will continue to grow forever.
He will rule as king on David's throne
    and over David's kingdom.
He will make it strong
    by ruling with justice and goodness
    from now on and forever.
The LORD All-Powerful will do this
    because of his strong love for his people.

The Word of the Lord.
Thanks be to God.

Pray now for your own needs and for the needs of others.

Allot ample time to freely express your prayers.

INTERCESSION

How wonderful are you, our God;
    How infinite is your wisdom.
You cover us with arms of grace;
    You protect us, your children.
Great are your ways, O Lord;
    Great, your unending love for us.
Forever we will offer you
    All of our praise.
For you are full of compassion
    And show mercy to your servants.

The disciples inquired, "Lord, teach us to pray." We join with his reply.

THE LORD'S PRAYER

Our Father, who art in heaven, hallowed be thy name. Thy Kingdom come, thy will be done, on earth as it is in heaven. Give us this day our daily bread. And forgive us our trespasses, as we forgive those who trespass against us. And lead us not into temptation, but deliver us from evil.

Spend a few moments in silence, meditating on the Lord.

CONCLUDING PRAYER

Everlasting God, you have been faithful in your promise to never leave us nor forsake us. May you set us apart this day to be holy, to be wholly yours, so that with each movement of the hours, our hearts will be drawn to you in loving prayer and honest devotion. In the blessed name of your Son, our Lord Jesus Christ, and in the fellowship of the Holy Spirit, amen.

2|13

DAY EIGHT

Quiet your heart before the Lord, then proceed as you feel ready.

LORD, open our lips,
  And our mouths shall proclaim your praise.

Glory to the Father, and to the Son, and to the Holy Spirit. As it was in the beginning, is now, and will be forever: from unending to unending. Amen.

For the mighty works of God, lift your praises.

PSALM 100
Jubilate Deo

Make a joyful noise unto the LORD, all ye lands.
Serve the LORD with gladness:
 come before his presence with singing.
Be joyful in the LORD, all you lands.
Know ye that the LORD he is God:
 it is he that hath made us, and not we ourselves;
 we are his people, and the sheep of his pasture.
Be joyful in the LORD, all you lands.
Enter into his gates with thanksgiving,
 and into his courts with praise:
 be thankful unto him, and bless his name.
Be joyful in the LORD, all you lands.
For the LORD is good; his mercy is everlasting;
 and his truth endureth to all generations.
His love and mercy endure forever.

Let us kneel and ask God to cleanse us from all unrighteousness.

PRAYER OF CONFESSION

Most holy and gracious God, we confess to you that we don't always get it right. We don't always love as you have called us to love. We don't often enough answer your invitation to serve. We don't continually seek the lost. But Father, you get it right with us every time. Accept our humble confession, and sanctify us by the power and beauty of your Word, that we may live in the light of your goodness, serve with the warmth of your gentleness, and love with the passion of your grace. Forever and ever, let it be so.

Pause for a moment to reflect on your repentance.

Then join with the psalmist's heart, giving praise and adoration.

PSALM 15
Domine, Quis Habitabit?

LORD, who shall abide in thy tabernacle?
  who shall dwell in thy holy hill?
He that walketh uprightly,
  and worketh righteousness,
  and speaketh the truth in his heart.
He that backbiteth not with his tongue,
  nor doeth evil to his neighbour,
  nor taketh up a reproach against his neighbour.
In whose eyes a vile person is contemned;
  but he honoureth them that fear the LORD.
  He that sweareth to his own hurt, and changeth not.
He that putteth not out his money to usury,
  nor taketh reward against the innocent.
  He that doeth these things
  shall never be moved.

Open your ears to hear the Word of the Lord.

A READING FROM SACRED SCRIPTURE
Ephesians 2:1–10 (The Message)

It wasn't so long ago that you were mired in that old stagnant life of sin. You let the world, which doesn't know the first thing about living, tell you how to live. You filled your lungs with polluted unbelief, and then exhaled disobedience. We all did it, all of us doing what we felt like doing, when we felt like doing it, all of us in the same boat. It's a wonder God didn't lose his temper and do away with the whole lot of us. Instead, immense in mercy and with an incredible love, he embraced us. He took our sin-dead lives and made us alive in Christ. He did all this on his own, with no help from us! Then he picked us up and set us down in highest heaven in company with Jesus, our Messiah.

Now God has us where he wants us, with all the time in this world and the next to shower grace and kindness upon us in Christ Jesus. Saving is all his idea, and all his work. All we do is trust him enough to let him do it. It's God's gift from start to finish! We don't play the major role. If we did, we'd probably go around bragging that we'd done the whole thing! No, we neither make nor save ourselves. God does both the making and saving. He creates each of us by Christ Jesus to join him in the work he does, the good work he has gotten ready for us to do, work we had better be doing.

> *The Word of the Lord.*
> *Thanks be to God.*

Pray now for your own needs and for the needs of others.

Allot ample time to freely express your prayers.

INTERCESSION

> Save your people, Lord, and bless your inheritance;
> *Govern and uphold them, now and always.*
> Day by day we bless you;
> *We praise your name forever.*
> Lord, keep us from all sin today;
> *Have mercy on us, Lord, have mercy.*
> Lord, show us your love and mercy;
> *For we put our trust in you.*
> In you, Lord, is our hope;
> *And we shall never hope in vain.*

The disciples inquired, "Lord, teach us to pray." We join with his reply.

THE LORD'S PRAYER

Our Father, who art in heaven, hallowed be thy name. Thy Kingdom come, thy will be done, on earth as it is in heaven. Give us this day our daily bread. And forgive us our trespasses, as we forgive those who trespass against us. And lead us not into temptation, but deliver us from evil.

Spend a few moments in silence, meditating on the Lord.

CONCLUDING PRAYER

Holy and Righteous Father, the world does not know you, nor does it desire to know you. Even so, you have revealed yourself to us through grace and mercy. Sanctify us by your truth—the truth of your Word—that we may be a strong light, shining your message of love and hope in this darkened world. In the blessed name of your Son, our Lord Jesus Christ, and in the fellowship of the Holy Spirit, amen.

2/14

DAY NINE

Quiet your heart before the Lord, then proceed as you feel ready.

May the words of our mouths
    And the meditations of our hearts
Be pleasing in your sight,
    O LORD, our Rock and our Redeemer.

Glory to the Father, and to the Son, and to the Holy Spirit. As it was in the beginning, is now, and will be forever: from unending to unending. Amen.

For the mighty works of God, lift your praises.

PSALM 147:1–9

Laudate Dominum

Praise ye the LORD:
> for it is good to sing praises unto our God;
> for it is pleasant; and praise is comely.

It is good to praise the LORD.

The LORD doth build up Jerusalem:
> he gathereth together the outcasts of Israel.

He healeth the broken in heart,
> and bindeth up their wounds.

The LORD is worthy of praise.

He telleth the number of the stars;
> he calleth them all by their names.

Great is our Lord, and of great power:
> his understanding is infinite.

The LORD lifteth up the meek:
> he casteth the wicked down to the ground.

Our God is great and mighty.

Sing unto the LORD with thanksgiving;
> sing praise upon the harp unto our God:

Who covereth the heaven with clouds,
> who prepareth rain for the earth,
> who maketh grass to grow upon the mountains.

He giveth to the beast his food,
> and to the young ravens which cry.

Sing to the LORD who provides.

Let us kneel and ask God to cleanse us from all unrighteousness.

PRAYER OF CONFESSION

Most holy and gracious God, we confess to you that we don't always get it right. We don't always love as you have called us to love. We don't often enough answer your invitation to serve. We don't continually seek the lost. But Father, you get it right with us every time. Accept our humble confession, and sanctify us by the power and beauty of your Word, that we may live in the light of your goodness, serve with the warmth of your gentleness, and love with the passion of your grace. Forever and ever, let it be so.

Pause for a moment to reflect on your repentance.

Then join with the psalmist's heart, giving praise and adoration.

PSALM 16:7–11
Conserva Me, Domine

I will bless the LORD, who hath given me counsel:
    my reins also instruct me in the night seasons.
I have set the LORD always before me:
    because he is at my right hand,
      I shall not be moved.
Therefore my heart is glad, and my glory rejoiceth:
    my flesh also shall rest in hope.
For thou wilt not leave my soul in hell;
    neither wilt thou suffer thine Holy One to see corruption.
Thou wilt shew me the path of life:
    in thy presence is fulness of joy;
    at thy right hand there are pleasures for evermore.

Open your ears to hear the Word of the Lord.

A READING FROM SACRED SCRIPTURE
Isaiah 11:1–9 (NCV)

A new branch will grow
    from a stump of a tree;
so a new king will come
    from the family of Jesse.
The Spirit of the LORD will rest upon that king.
    The Spirit will give him wisdom and understanding,
      guidance and power.
    The Spirit will teach him to know and respect the LORD.
This king will be glad to obey the LORD.

He will not judge by the way things look
   or decide by what he hears.
But he will judge the poor honestly;
   he will be fair in his decisions for the poor people of the land.
At his command evil people will be punished,
   and by his words the wicked will be put to death.
Goodness and fairness will give him strength,
   like a belt around his waist.
Then wolves will live in peace with lambs,
   and leopards will lie down to rest with goats.
Calves, lions, and young bulls will eat together,
   and a little child will lead them.
Cows and bears will eat together in peace.
   Their young will lie down to rest together.
   Lions will eat hay as oxen do.
A baby will be able to play near a cobra's hole,
   and a child will be able to put his hand into the nest of a
      poisonous snake.
They will not hurt or destroy each other
   on all my holy mountain,
because the earth will be full of the knowledge of the LORD,
   as the sea is full of water.

The Word of the Lord.
Thanks be to God.

Pray now for your own needs and for the needs of others.

Allot ample time to freely express your prayers.

INTERCESSION

We will exalt your name, O Lord,
   For you have heard our cries,
And you have healed us.
   The Lord has lifted us up from the depths.
We will sing praises to you our Lord,
   For your anger is fleeting,

But your favor lasts forever.
> *The Lord has lifted us up from the depths.*

Our hearts cannot stay silent,
Forever we will give you thanks.
> *The Lord has lifted us up from the depths.*

The disciples inquired, "Lord, teach us to pray." We join with his reply.

THE LORD'S PRAYER

Our Father, who art in heaven, hallowed be thy name. Thy Kingdom come, thy will be done, on earth as it is in heaven. Give us this day our daily bread. And forgive us our trespasses, as we forgive those who trespass against us. And lead us not into temptation, but deliver us from evil.

Spend a few moments in silence, meditating on the Lord.

CONCLUDING PRAYER

Holy and Righteous Father, the world does not know you, nor does it desire to know you. Even so, you have revealed yourself to us through grace and mercy. Sanctify us by your truth—the truth of your Word—that we may be a strong light, shining your message of love and hope in this darkened world. In the blessed name of your Son, our Lord Jesus Christ, and in the fellowship of the Holy Spirit, amen.

Quiet your heart before the Lord, then proceed as you feel ready.

Teach us your way, O LORD,
>And we will walk in your truth.
Give us undivided hearts,
>That we may fear your name.

Glory to the Father, and to the Son, and to the Holy Spirit. As it was in the beginning, is now, and will be forever: from unending to unending. Amen.

For the mighty works of God, lift your praises.

PSALM 149:1–4

Cantate Domino

Praise ye the LORD.
>Sing unto the LORD a new song,
>and his praise in the congregation of saints.
Sing to the LORD a new song.
Let Israel rejoice in him that made him:
>let the children of Zion be joyful in their King.
Let them praise his name in the dance:
>let them sing praises unto him with the timbrel and harp.
Make music for the LORD our God.
For the LORD taketh pleasure in his people:
>he will beautify the meek with salvation.
For the LORD saves us.

Let us kneel and ask God to cleanse us from all unrighteousness.

PRAYER OF CONFESSION

Most holy and gracious God, we confess to you that we don't always get it right. We don't always love as you have called us to love. We don't often enough answer your invitation to serve. We don't continually seek the lost. But Father, you get it right with us every time. Accept our humble confession, and sanctify us by the power and beauty of your Word, that we may live in the light of your goodness, serve with the warmth of your gentleness, and love with the passion of your grace. Forever and ever, let it be so.

Pause for a moment to reflect on your repentance.

Then join with the psalmist's heart, giving praise and adoration.

PSALM 18:1–6
Diligam Te, Domine

I will love thee, O Lord, my strength.
The Lord is my rock, and my fortress, and my deliverer;
 my God, my strength, in whom I will trust;
 my buckler, and the horn of my salvation, and my high tower.
I will call upon the Lord, who is worthy to be praised:
 so shall I be saved from mine enemies.
The sorrows of death compassed me,
 and the floods of ungodly men made me afraid.
The sorrows of hell compassed me about:
 the snares of death prevented me.
In my distress I called upon the Lord,
 and cried unto my God:
 he heard my voice out of his temple,
 and my cry came before him, even into his ears.

Open your ears to hear the Word of the Lord.

A READING FROM SACRED SCRIPTURE
Isaiah 25:1–8 (NCV)

LORD, you are my God.
  I honor you and praise you,
because you have done amazing things.
    You have always done what you said you would do;
    you have done what you planned long ago.
You have made the city a pile of rocks
    and have destroyed her walls.
The city our enemies built with strong walls is gone;
    it will never be built again.
People from powerful nations will honor you;
    cruel people from strong cities will fear you.
You protect the poor;
    you protect the helpless when they are in danger.
You are like a shelter from storms,
    like shade that protects them from the heat.
The cruel people attack
    like a rainstorm beating against the wall,
    like the heat in the desert.
But you, God, stop their violent attack.
    As a cloud cools a hot day,
    you silence the songs of those who have no mercy.
The LORD All-Powerful will prepare a feast
    on this mountain for all people.
It will be a feast with all the best food and wine,
    the finest meat and wine.
On this mountain God will destroy
    the veil that covers all nations,
the veil that stretches over all peoples;
    he will destroy death forever.
The Lord GOD will wipe away every tear from every face.
    He will take away the shame of his people from the earth.
The LORD has spoken.

The Word of the Lord.
Thanks be to God.

Pray now for your own needs and for the needs of others.

Allot ample time to freely express your prayers.

INTERCESSION

The earth is yours and everything in it,
King of Glory, hear our prayers.
You founded it upon the sea, upon the waters;
King of Glory, hear our prayers.
You clean our hands from the dirt of our sin;
King of Glory, hear our prayers.
You lead us up the mountain, your holy hill;
King of Glory, hear our prayers.
Who is this King of Glory?
The Lord Almighty—he will hear our prayers.

The disciples inquired, "Lord, teach us to pray." We join with his reply.

THE LORD'S PRAYER

Our Father, who art in heaven, hallowed be thy name. Thy Kingdom come, thy will be done, on earth as it is in heaven. Give us this day our daily bread. And forgive us our trespasses, as we forgive those who trespass against us. And lead us not into temptation, but deliver us from evil.

Spend a few moments in silence, meditating on the Lord.

CONCLUDING PRAYER

Holy and Righteous Father, the world does not know you, nor does it desire to know you. Even so, you have revealed yourself to us through grace and mercy. Sanctify us by your truth—the truth of your Word—that we may be a strong light, shining your message of love and hope in this darkened world. In the blessed name of your Son, our Lord Jesus Christ, and in the fellowship of the Holy Spirit, amen.

Quiet your heart before the Lord, then proceed as you feel ready.

Give thanks to the LORD,
    And call upon his name.
Make known among the nations
    The great works he has done.

Glory to the Father, and to the Son, and to the Holy Spirit. As it was in the beginning, is now, and will be forever: from unending to unending. Amen.

For the mighty works of God, lift your praises.

PSALM 95:1–7
Venite Exultemus

O come, let us sing unto the LORD:
    let us make a joyful noise to the rock of our salvation.
Let us come before his presence with thanksgiving,
    and make a joyful noise unto him with psalms.
Let us shout to the Rock.
For the LORD is a great God,
    and a great King above all gods.

In his hand are the deep places of the earth:
>the strength of the hills is his also.

The sea is his, and he made it:
>and his hands formed the dry land.

Let us worship our Lord, our Creator.

O come, let us worship and bow down:
>let us kneel before the LORD our maker.

For he is our God;
>and we are the people of his pasture,
>and the sheep of his hand.

For he is the Great Shepherd.

Let us kneel and ask God to cleanse us from all unrighteousness.

PRAYER OF CONFESSION

Most holy and gracious God, we confess to you that we don't always get it right. We don't always love as you have called us to love. We don't often enough answer your invitation to serve. We don't continually seek the lost. But Father, you get it right with us every time. Accept our humble confession, and sanctify us by the power and beauty of your Word, that we may live in the light of your goodness, serve with the warmth of your gentleness, and love with the passion of your grace. Forever and ever, let it be so.

Pause for a moment to reflect on your repentance.

Then join with the psalmist's heart, giving praise and adoration.

PSALM 19:1–8
Caeli Enarrant

The heavens declare the glory of God;
>and the firmament sheweth his handywork.

Day unto day uttereth speech,
>and night unto night sheweth knowledge.

There is no speech nor language,
>where their voice is not heard.

Their line is gone out through all the earth,
    and their words to the end of the world.
    In them hath he set a tabernacle for the sun,
Which is as a bridegroom coming out of his chamber,
    and rejoiceth as a strong man to run a race.
His going forth is from the end of the heaven,
    and his circuit unto the ends of it:
    and there is nothing hid from the heat thereof.
The law of the LORD is perfect,
    converting the soul:
    the testimony of the LORD is sure,
    making wise the simple.
The statutes of the LORD are right,
    rejoicing the heart:
    the commandment of the LORD is pure,
    enlightening the eyes.

Open your ears to hear the Word of the Lord.

A READING FROM SACRED SCRIPTURE
Romans 3:9–26 (NIV)

What shall we conclude then? Are we any better? Not at all! We have already made the charge that Jews and Gentiles alike are all under sin. As it is written: "There is no one righteous, not even one; there is no one who understands, no one who seeks God. All have turned away, they have together become worthless; there is no one who does good, not even one. Their throats are open graves; their tongues practice deceit. The poison of vipers is on their lips. Their mouths are full of cursing and bitterness. Their feet are swift to shed blood; ruin and misery mark their ways, and the way of peace they do not know. There is no fear of God before their eyes."

Now we know that whatever the law says, it says to those who are under the law, so that every mouth may be silenced and the whole world held accountable to God. Therefore no one will be declared righteous in his sight by observing the law; rather, through the law we become conscious of sin.

But now a righteousness from God, apart from law, has been made known, to which the Law and the Prophets testify. This righteousness from God comes through faith in Jesus Christ to all who believe. There is no difference, for all have sinned and fall short of the glory of God, and are justified freely by his grace through the redemption that came by Christ Jesus. God presented him as a sacrifice of atonement, through faith in his blood. He did this to demonstrate his justice, because in his forbearance he had left the sins committed beforehand unpunished—he did it to demonstrate his justice at the present time, so as to be just and the one who justifies those who have faith in Jesus.

The Word of the Lord.
Thanks be to God.

Pray now for your own needs and for the needs of others.

Allot ample time to freely express your prayers.

INTERCESSION

Blessed are the poor in spirit,
For theirs is the kingdom of heaven.
Blessed are those who mourn,
For they will be comforted.
Blessed are the meek,
For they will inherit the earth.
Blessed are those who hunger for righteousness,
For they will be filled.
Blessed are the merciful,
For they will be shown mercy.
Blessed are the pure in heart,
For they will see God.
Blessed are the peacemakers,
For they will be called sons of God.

The disciples inquired, "Lord, teach us to pray." We join with his reply.

THE LORD'S PRAYER

Our Father, who art in heaven, hallowed be thy name. Thy Kingdom come, thy will be done, on earth as it is in heaven. Give us this day our daily bread. And forgive us our trespasses, as we forgive those who trespass against us. And lead us not into temptation, but deliver us from evil.

Spend a few moments in silence, meditating on the Lord.

CONCLUDING PRAYER

Holy and Righteous Father, the world does not know you, nor does it desire to know you. Even so, you have revealed yourself to us through grace and mercy. Sanctify us by your truth—the truth of your Word—that we may be a strong light, shining your message of love and hope in this darkened world. In the blessed name of your Son, our Lord Jesus Christ, and in the fellowship of the Holy Spirit, amen.

DAY TWELVE

Quiet your heart before the Lord, then proceed as you feel ready.

From the rising of the sun,
    The name of the LORD is to be praised.
To the place where it sets,
    The name of the LORD is to be praised.

Glory to the Father, and to the Son, and to the Holy Spirit. As it was in the beginning, is now, and will be forever: from unending to unending. Amen.

For the mighty works of God, lift your praises.

PSALM 146:1–8
Lauda, Anima Mea

Praise ye the LORD.
  Praise the LORD, O my soul.
While I live will I praise the LORD:
  I will sing praises unto my God while I have any being.
Praise the LORD, O my soul.
Put not your trust in princes,
  nor in the son of man, in whom there is no help.
His breath goeth forth, he returneth to his earth;
  in that very day his thoughts perish.
Praise the LORD, O my soul.
Happy is he that hath the God of Jacob for his help,
  whose hope is in the LORD his God:
Which made heaven, and earth,
  the sea, and all that therein is:
  which keepeth truth for ever:
Praise the LORD, O my soul.
Which executeth judgment for the oppressed:
  which giveth food to the hungry.
The LORD looseth the prisoners:
The LORD openeth the eyes of the blind:
  the LORD raiscth them that are bowed down:
  the LORD loveth the righteous:

Praise the Lord, O my soul.

Let us kneel and ask God to cleanse us from all unrighteousness.

PRAYER OF CONFESSION

Most holy and gracious God, we confess to you that we don't always get it right. We don't always love as you have called us to love. We don't often enough answer your invitation to serve. We don't continually seek the lost. But Father, you get it right with us every time. Accept our humble confession, and sanctify us by the power and beauty of your Word, that we may live in the light of your goodness, serve with the warmth of your gentleness, and love with the passion of your grace. Forever and ever, let it be so.

Pause for a moment to reflect on your repentance.

Then join with the psalmist's heart, giving praise and adoration.

PSALM 22:1–5
Deus, Deus Meus

My God, my God, why hast thou forsaken me?
> why art thou so far from helping me,
> and from the words of my roaring?

O my God, I cry in the daytime, but thou hearest not;
> and in the night season, and am not silent.

But thou art holy,
> O thou that inhabitest the praises of Israel.

Our fathers trusted in thee:
> they trusted, and thou didst deliver them.

They cried unto thee, and were delivered:
> they trusted in thee, and were not confounded.

Open your ears to hear the Word of the Lord.

A READING FROM SACRED SCRIPTURE
Isaiah 26:12–19 (NCV)

LORD, all our success is because of what you have done,
> so give us peace.

LORD, our God, other masters besides you have ruled us,

but we honor only you.
Those masters are now dead;
   their ghosts will not rise from death.
You punished and destroyed them
   and erased any memory of them.
LORD, you multiplied the number of your people;
   you multiplied them and brought honor to yourself.
You made the borders of the land wide.
LORD, people remember you when they are in trouble;
   they say quiet prayers to you when you punish them.
LORD, when we are with you,
   we are like a woman giving birth to a baby;
   she cries and has pain from the birth.
In the same way, we had pain.
   We gave birth, but only to wind.
We don't bring salvation to the land
   or make new people for the world.
Your people have died, but they will live again;
   their bodies will rise from death.
You who lie in the ground,
   wake up and be happy!
The dew covering you is like the dew of a new day;
   the ground will give birth to the dead.

The Word of the Lord.
Thanks be to God.

Pray now for your own needs and for the needs of others.

Allot ample time to freely express your prayers.

INTERCESSION

Cleanse me with hyssop, and I will be clean;
   Wash me, and I will be whiter than snow.
Hide your face from my sins
   And blot out all my iniquity.

Create in me a pure heart, O God,
And renew a steadfast spirit within me.
Do not cast me from your presence
Or take your Holy Spirit from me.
Restore to me the joy of your salvation
And grant me a willing spirit, to sustain me.

The disciples inquired, "Lord, teach us to pray." We join with his reply.

THE LORD'S PRAYER

Our Father, who art in heaven, hallowed be thy name. Thy Kingdom come, thy will be done, on earth as it is in heaven. Give us this day our daily bread. And forgive us our trespasses, as we forgive those who trespass against us. And lead us not into temptation, but deliver us from evil.

Spend a few moments in silence, meditating on the Lord.

CONCLUDING PRAYER

Holy and Righteous Father, the world does not know you, nor does it desire to know you. Even so, you have revealed yourself to us through grace and mercy. Sanctify us by your truth—the truth of your Word—that we may be a strong light, shining your message of love and hope in this darkened world. In the blessed name of your Son, our Lord Jesus Christ, and in the fellowship of the Holy Spirit, amen.

Quiet your heart before the Lord, then proceed as you feel ready.

Love the LORD,
    All you his saints.
Love the LORD your God,
    All you his faithful.

Glory to the Father, and to the Son, and to the Holy Spirit. As it was in the beginning, is now, and will be forever: from unending to unending. Amen.

For the mighty works of God, lift your praises.

PSALM 67
Deus Misereatur

God be merciful unto us, and bless us;
    and cause his face to shine upon us;
    Selah.
That thy way may be known upon earth,
    thy saving health among all nations.
O God, shine upon us.
Let the people praise thee, O God;
    let all the people praise thee.
O let the nations be glad and sing for joy:
    for thou shalt judge the people righteously,
    and govern the nations upon earth.
    Selah.
Let the people praise thee, O God;

let all the people praise thee.
O God, may we, your people, praise you.
Then shall the earth yield her increase;
and God, even our own God, shall bless us.
God shall bless us;
and all the ends of the earth shall fear him.
O God, may we, your people, praise you.

Let us kneel and ask God to cleanse us from all unrighteousness.

PRAYER OF CONFESSION

Most holy and gracious God, we confess to you that we don't always get it right. We don't always love as you have called us to love. We don't often enough answer your invitation to serve. We don't continually seek the lost. But Father, you get it right with us every time. Accept our humble confession, and sanctify us by the power and beauty of your Word, that we may live in the light of your goodness, serve with the warmth of your gentleness, and love with the passion of your grace. Forever and ever, let it be so.

Pause for a moment to reflect on your repentance.

Then join with the psalmist's heart, giving praise and adoration.

PSALM 23
Dominus Regit Me

The LORD is my shepherd; I shall not want.
He maketh me to lie down in green pastures:
he leadeth me beside the still waters.
He restoreth my soul:
he leadeth me in the paths of righteousness
for his name's sake.
Yea, though I walk
through the valley of the shadow of death,
I will fear no evil:
for thou art with me;

thy rod and thy staff
they comfort me.
Thou preparest a table before me
in the presence of mine enemies:
thou anointest my head with oil; my cup runneth over.
Surely goodness and mercy shall follow me
all the days of my life:
and I will dwell in the house of the LORD
for ever.

Open your ears to hear the Word of the Lord.

A READING FROM SACRED SCRIPTURE
Romans 4:1–17 (NIV)

What then shall we say that Abraham, our forefather, discovered in this matter? If, in fact, Abraham was justified by works, he had something to boast about—but not before God. What does the Scripture say? "Abraham believed God, and it was credited to him as righteousness."

Now when a man works, his wages are not credited to him as a gift, but as an obligation. However, to the man who does not work but trusts God who justifies the wicked, his faith is credited as righteousness. David says the same thing when he speaks of the blessedness of the man to whom God credits righteousness apart from works:

"Blessed are they
whose transgressions are forgiven,
whose sins are covered.
Blessed is the man
whose sin the Lord will never count against him."

Is this blessedness only for the circumcised, or also for the uncircumcised? We have been saying that Abraham's faith was credited to him as righteousness. Under what circumstances was it credited? Was it after he was circumcised, or before? It was not after, but before! And he received the sign of circumcision, a seal of the righteousness that he had by faith while he was still uncircumcised. So then, he is the father of all who believe but have not been circumcised, in order that righteousness might be credited to them. And he is also the father of the circumcised who not only are circumcised but who also walk in the footsteps of the faith that our father Abraham had before he was circumcised.

It was not through law that Abraham and his offspring received the promise that he would be heir of the world, but through the righteousness that comes by faith. For if those who live by law are heirs, faith has no value and the promise is worthless, because law brings wrath. And where there is no law there is no transgression.

Therefore, the promise comes by faith, so that it may be by grace and may be guaranteed to all Abraham's offspring — not only to those who are of the law but also to those who are of the faith of Abraham. He is the father of us all. As it is written: "I have made you a father of many nations." He is our father in the sight of God, in whom he believed — the God who gives life to the dead and calls things that are not as though they were.

The Word of the Lord.
Thanks be to God.

Pray now for your own needs and for the needs of others.

Allot ample time to freely express your prayers.

INTERCESSION

Show us your mercy, O Lord;
And grant us your salvation.
Clothe your ministers with righteousness;
Let your people sing with joy.
Give peace, O Lord, in all the world;
For only in you can we live in safety.
Lord, keep this nation under your care;

And guide us in the way of justice and truth.
Let your way be known upon earth;
Your saving health among all nations.
Let not the needy, O Lord, be forgotten;
Nor the hope of the poor be taken away.
Create in us clean hearts, O God;
And sustain us with your Holy Spirit.

The disciples inquired, "Lord, teach us to pray." We join with his reply.

THE LORD'S PRAYER

Our Father, who art in heaven, hallowed be thy name. Thy Kingdom come, thy will be done, on earth as it is in heaven. Give us this day our daily bread. And forgive us our trespasses, as we forgive those who trespass against us. And lead us not into temptation, but deliver us from evil.

Spend a few moments in silence, meditating on the Lord.

CONCLUDING PRAYER

Holy and Righteous Father, the world does not know you, nor does it desire to know you. Even so, you have revealed yourself to us through grace and mercy. Sanctify us by your truth—the truth of your Word—that we may be a strong light, shining your message of love and hope in this darkened world. In the blessed name of your Son, our Lord Jesus Christ, and in the fellowship of the Holy Spirit, amen.

DAY FOURTEEN

Quiet your heart before the Lord, then proceed as you feel ready.

Ascribe to the LORD
　The glory due his name.
Worship the LORD
　In the splendor of his holiness.

Glory to the Father, and to the Son, and to the Holy Spirit. As it was in the beginning, is now, and will be forever: from unending to unending. Amen.

For the mighty works of God, lift your praises.

PSALM 148:1–12
Laudate Dominum

Praise ye the LORD.
　Praise ye the LORD from the heavens:
　praise him in the heights.
Praise ye him, all his angels:
　praise ye him, all his hosts.
Let us praise the LORD.
Praise ye him, sun and moon:
　praise him, all ye stars of light.
Praise him, ye heavens of heavens,
　and ye waters that be above the heavens.
Let them praise the name of the LORD:
　for he commanded, and they were created.
He hath also stablished them for ever and ever:
　he hath made a decree which shall not pass.

Let them praise the LORD.
Praise the LORD from the earth,
    ye dragons, and all deeps:
Fire, and hail; snow, and vapour;
    stormy wind fulfilling his word:
Mountains, and all hills;
    fruitful trees, and all cedars:
Beasts, and all cattle;
    creeping things, and flying fowl:
Kings of the earth, and all people;
    princes, and all judges of the earth:
Both young men, and maidens;
    old men, and children:

Let all voices praise the LORD.

Let us kneel and ask God to cleanse us from all unrighteousness.

PRAYER OF CONFESSION

Most holy and gracious God, we confess to you that we don't always get it right. We don't always love as you have called us to love. We don't often enough answer your invitation to serve. We don't continually seek the lost. But Father, you get it right with us every time. Accept our humble confession, and sanctify us by the power and beauty of your Word, that we may live in the light of your goodness, serve with the warmth of your gentleness, and love with the passion of your grace. Forever and ever, let it be so.

Pause for a moment to reflect on your repentance.

Then join with the psalmist's heart, giving praise and adoration.

PSALM 24
Domini Est Terra

The earth is the LORD's, and the fulness thereof;
    the world, and they that dwell therein.
For he hath founded it upon the seas,

and established it upon the floods.
Who shall ascend into the hill of the LORD?
    or who shall stand in his holy place?
He that hath clean hands, and a pure heart;
    who hath not lifted up his soul unto vanity,
    nor sworn deceitfully.
He shall receive the blessing from the LORD,
    and righteousness from the God of his salvation.
This is the generation of them that seek him,
    that seek thy face, O Jacob.
    Selah.
Lift up your heads, O ye gates;
    and be ye lifted up, ye everlasting doors;
    and the King of glory shall come in.
Who is this King of glory?
    The LORD strong and mighty,
    the LORD mighty in battle.
Lift up your heads, O ye gates;
    even lift them up, ye everlasting doors;
    and the King of glory shall come in.
Who is this King of glory?
    The LORD of hosts,
    he is the King of glory.
    Selah.

Open your ears to hear the Word of the Lord.

A READING FROM SACRED SCRIPTURE
Isaiah 28:16–21 (NCV)

Because of these things, this is what the Lord GOD says:
"I will put a stone in the ground in Jerusalem,
    a tested stone.
Everything will be built on this important and precious rock.
    Anyone who trusts in it will never be disappointed.
I will use justice as a measuring line
    and goodness as the standard.

The lies you hide behind will be destroyed as if by hail.
  They will be washed away as if in a flood.
Your agreement with death will be erased;
  your contract with death will not help you.
When terrible punishment comes,
  you will be crushed by it.
Whenever punishment comes, it will take you away.
  It will come morning after morning;
  it will defeat you by day and by night.
Those who understand this punishment will be terrified."
You will be like the person who tried to sleep
  on a bed that was too short
and with a blanket that was too narrow
  to wrap around himself.
The LORD will fight as he did at Mount Perazim.
  He will be angry as he was in the Valley of Gibeon.
He will do his work, his strange work.
  He will finish his job, his strange job.

The Word of the Lord.
Thanks be to God.

Pray now for your own needs and for the needs of others.

Allot ample time to freely express your prayers.

INTERCESSION

How wonderful are you, our God;
  How infinite is your wisdom.
You cover us with arms of grace;
  You protect us, your children.
Great are your ways, O Lord;
  Great, your unending love for us.
Forever we will offer you
  All of our praise.
For you are full of compassion
  And show mercy to your servants.

The disciples inquired, "Lord, teach us to pray." We join with his reply.

THE LORD'S PRAYER

Our Father, who art in heaven, hallowed be thy name. Thy Kingdom come, thy will be done, on earth as it is in heaven. Give us this day our daily bread. And forgive us our trespasses, as we forgive those who trespass against us. And lead us not into temptation, but deliver us from evil.

Spend a few moments in silence, meditating on the Lord.

CONCLUDING PRAYER

Holy and Righteous Father, the world does not know you, nor does it desire to know you. Even so, you have revealed yourself to us through grace and mercy. Sanctify us by your truth—the truth of your Word—that we may be a strong light, shining your message of love and hope in this darkened world. In the blessed name of your Son, our Lord Jesus Christ, and in the fellowship of the Holy Spirit, amen.

2/20

DAY FIFTEEN

DAY FIFTEEN

Quiet your heart before the Lord, then proceed as you feel ready.

LORD, open our lips,
    And our mouths shall proclaim your praise.

Glory to the Father, and to the Son, and to the Holy Spirit. As it was in the beginning, is now, and will be forever: from unending to unending. Amen.

For the mighty works of God, lift your praises.

PSALM 100
Jubilate Deo

Make a joyful noise unto the LORD, all ye lands.
Serve the LORD with gladness:
  come before his presence with singing.
Be joyful in the LORD, all you lands.
Know ye that the LORD he is God:
  it is he that hath made us, and not we ourselves;
  we are his people, and the sheep of his pasture.
Be joyful in the LORD, all you lands.
Enter into his gates with thanksgiving,
  and into his courts with praise:
  be thankful unto him, and bless his name.
Be joyful in the LORD, all you lands.
For the LORD is good; his mercy is everlasting;
  and his truth endureth to all generations.
His love and mercy endure forever.

Let us kneel and ask God to cleanse us from all unrighteousness.

PRAYER OF CONFESSION

Most holy and gracious God, we confess to you that we don't always get it right. We don't always love as you have called us to love. We don't often enough answer your invitation to serve. We don't continually seek the lost. But Father, you get it right with us every time. Accept our humble confession, and sanctify us by the power and beauty of your Word, that we may live in the light of your goodness, serve with the warmth of your gentleness, and love with the passion of your grace. Forever and ever, let it be so.

Pause for a moment to reflect on your repentance.

Then join with the psalmist's heart, giving praise and adoration.

PSALM 25:1–7
Ad Te, Domine, Levavi

Unto thee, O LORD, do I lift up my soul.
O my God, I trust in thee:
    let me not be ashamed,
    let not mine enemies triumph over me.
Yea, let none that wait on thee
    be ashamed:
    let them be ashamed
    which transgress without cause.
Shew me thy ways, O LORD;
    teach me thy paths.
Lead me in thy truth, and teach me:
    for thou art the God of my salvation;
    on thee do I wait all the day.
Remember, O LORD,
    thy tender mercies and thy lovingkindnesses;
    for they have been ever of old.
Remember not the sins of my youth,
    nor my transgressions:
    according to thy mercy remember thou me
    for thy goodness' sake, O LORD.

Open your ears to hear the Word of the Lord.

A READING FROM SACRED SCRIPTURE
Ephesians 3:14–21 (The Message)

My response is to get down on my knees before the Father, this magnificent Father who parcels out all heaven and earth. I ask him to strengthen you by his Spirit—not a brute strength but a glorious inner strength—that Christ will live in you as you open the door and invite him in. And I ask him that with both feet planted firmly on love, you'll be able to take in with all followers of Jesus the extravagant dimensions of Christ's love. Reach out and experience the breadth! Test its length! Plumb the depths! Rise to the heights! Live full lives, full in the fullness of God.

God can do anything, you know—far more than you could ever imagine or guess or request in your wildest dreams! He does it not by pushing us around but by working within us, his Spirit deeply and gently within us.

Glory to God in the church!
Glory to God in the Messiah, in Jesus!
Glory down all the generations!
Glory through all millennia! Oh, yes!

The Word of the Lord.
Thanks be to God.

Pray now for your own needs and for the needs of others.

Allot ample time to freely express your prayers.

INTERCESSION

Save your people, Lord, and bless your inheritance;
Govern and uphold them, now and always.
Day by day we bless you;
We praise your name forever.
Lord, keep us from all sin today;
Have mercy on us, Lord, have mercy.
Lord, show us your love and mercy;
For we put our trust in you.
In you, Lord, is our hope;
And we shall never hope in vain.

The disciples inquired, "Lord, teach us to pray." We join with his reply.

THE LORD'S PRAYER

Our Father, who art in heaven, hallowed be thy name. Thy Kingdom come, thy will be done, on earth as it is in heaven. Give us this day our daily bread. And forgive us our trespasses, as we forgive those who trespass against us. And lead us not into temptation, but deliver us from evil.

Spend a few moments in silence, meditating on the Lord.

CONCLUDING PRAYER

Glorious Father, may you strengthen us deep within our spirits, through your most Holy Spirit—that Christ may dwell in our hearts through faith, giving us the power to grasp the height and depth and breadth of your unending love. And on this day, may we be filled to the measure of all the fullness of who you are. In the blessed name of your Son, our Lord Jesus Christ, and in the fellowship of the Holy Spirit, amen.

DAY SIXTEEN

Quiet your heart before the Lord, then proceed as you feel ready.

May the words of our mouths
 And the meditations of our hearts
Be pleasing in your sight,
 O LORD, our Rock and our Redeemer.

Glory to the Father, and to the Son, and to the Holy Spirit. As it was in the beginning, is now, and will be forever: from unending to unending. Amen.

For the mighty works of God, lift your praises.

PSALM 147:1–9
Laudate Dominum

Praise ye the LORD:
> for it is good to sing praises unto our God;
> for it is pleasant; and praise is comely.

It is good to praise the LORD.

The LORD doth build up Jerusalem:
> he gathereth together the outcasts of Israel.

He healeth the broken in heart,
> and bindeth up their wounds.

The LORD is worthy of praise.

He telleth the number of the stars;
> he calleth them all by their names.

Great is our Lord, and of great power:
> his understanding is infinite.

The LORD lifteth up the meek:
> he casteth the wicked down to the ground.

Our God is great and mighty.

Sing unto the LORD with thanksgiving;
> sing praise upon the harp unto our God:

Who covereth the heaven with clouds,
> who prepareth rain for the earth,
> who maketh grass to grow upon the mountains.

He giveth to the beast his food,
> and to the young ravens which cry.

Sing to the LORD who provides.

Let us kneel and ask God to cleanse us from all unrighteousness.

PRAYER OF CONFESSION

Most holy and gracious God, we confess to you that we don't always get it right. We don't always love as you have called us to love. We don't often enough answer your invitation to serve. We don't continually seek the lost. But Father, you get it right with us every time. Accept our humble confession, and sanctify us by the power and beauty of your Word, that we may live in the light of your goodness, serve with the warmth of your gentleness, and love with the passion of your grace. Forever and ever, let it be so.

Pause for a moment to reflect on your repentance.

Then join with the psalmist's heart, giving praise and adoration.

PSALM 27:1–6
Dominus Illuminatio

The LORD is my light and my salvation;
>   whom shall I fear?
>   the LORD is the strength of my life;
>   of whom shall I be afraid?
When the wicked, even mine enemies and my foes,
>   came upon me to eat up my flesh,
>   they stumbled and fell.
Though an host should encamp against me,
>   my heart shall not fear:
>   though war should rise against me,
>   in this will I be confident.
One thing have I desired of the LORD,
>   that will I seek after;
>   that I may dwell in the house of the LORD
>   all the days of my life,
>   to behold the beauty of the LORD,
>   and to enquire in his temple.
For in the time of trouble
>   he shall hide me in his pavilion:

in the secret of his tabernacle shall he hide me;
    he shall set me up upon a rock.
And now shall mine head be lifted up
    above mine enemies round about me:
    therefore will I offer in his tabernacle sacrifices of joy;
    I will sing, yea,
    I will sing praises unto the LORD.

Open your ears to hear the Word of the Lord.

A READING FROM SACRED SCRIPTURE
Isaiah 30:15–21 (NCV)

This is what the Lord GOD, the Holy One of Israel, says:
"If you come back to me and trust me, you will be saved.
    If you will be calm and trust me, you will be strong."
    But you don't want to do that.
You say, "No, we need horses to run away on."
    So you will run away on horses.
You say, "We will ride away on fast horses."
    So those who chase you will be fast.
One enemy will make threats,
    and a thousand of your men will run away.
Five enemies will make threats,
    and all of you will run from them.
You will be left alone like a flagpole on a hilltop,
    like a banner on a hill.
The LORD wants to show his mercy to you.
    He wants to rise and comfort you.
The LORD is a fair God,
    and everyone who waits for his help will be happy.
You people who live on Mount Zion in Jerusalem will not cry
anymore. The LORD will hear your crying, and he will comfort you.
When he hears you, he will help you. The Lord has given you sor-
row and hurt like the bread and water you ate every day. He is your
teacher; he will not continue to hide from you, but you will see your
teacher with your own eyes. If you go the wrong way—to the right

or to the left—you will hear a voice behind you saying, "This is the right way. You should go this way."

The Word of the Lord.
Thanks be to God.

Pray now for your own needs and for the needs of others.

Allot ample time to freely express your prayers.

INTERCESSION

We will exalt your name, O Lord,
For you have heard our cries,
And you have healed us.
The Lord has lifted us up from the depths.
We will sing praises to you our Lord,
For your anger is fleeting,
But your favor lasts forever.
The Lord has lifted us up from the depths.
Our hearts cannot stay silent,
Forever we will give you thanks.
The Lord has lifted us up from the depths.

The disciples inquired, "Lord, teach us to pray." We join with his reply.

THE LORD'S PRAYER

Our Father, who art in heaven, hallowed be thy name. Thy Kingdom come, thy will be done, on earth as it is in heaven. Give us this day our daily bread. And forgive us our trespasses, as we forgive those who trespass against us. And lead us not into temptation, but deliver us from evil.

Spend a few moments in silence, meditating on the Lord.

CONCLUDING PRAYER

Glorious Father, may you strengthen us deep within our spirits, through your most Holy Spirit—that Christ may dwell in our hearts through faith, giving us the power to grasp the height and depth and breadth of your unending love. And on this day, may we be filled to the measure of all the fullness of who you are. In the blessed name of your Son, our Lord Jesus Christ, and in the fellowship of the Holy Spirit, amen.

DAY SEVENTEEN

Quiet your heart before the Lord, then proceed as you feel ready.

Teach us your way, O LORD,
    And we will walk in your truth.
Give us undivided hearts,
    That we may fear your name.

Glory to the Father, and to the Son, and to the Holy Spirit. As it was in the beginning, is now, and will be forever: from unending to unending. Amen.

For the mighty works of God, lift your praises.

PSALM 149:1–4
Cantate Domino

    Praise ye the LORD.
        Sing unto the LORD a new song,

and his praise in the congregation of saints.
Sing to the LORD a new song.
Let Israel rejoice in him that made him:
    let the children of Zion be joyful in their King.
Let them praise his name in the dance:
    let them sing praises unto him with the timbrel and harp.
Make music for the LORD our God.
For the LORD taketh pleasure in his people:
    he will beautify the meek with salvation.
For the LORD saves us.

Let us kneel and ask God to cleanse us from all unrighteousness.

PRAYER OF CONFESSION

Most holy and gracious God, we confess to you that we don't always get it right. We don't always love as you have called us to love. We don't often enough answer your invitation to serve. We don't continually seek the lost. But Father, you get it right with us every time. Accept our humble confession, and sanctify us by the power and beauty of your Word, that we may live in the light of your goodness, serve with the warmth of your gentleness, and love with the passion of your grace. Forever and ever, let it be so.

Pause for a moment to reflect on your repentance.

Then join with the psalmist's heart, giving praise and adoration.

PSALM 29

Afferte Domino

Give unto the LORD, O ye mighty,
    give unto the LORD glory and strength.
Give unto the LORD the glory due unto his name;
    worship the LORD in the beauty of holiness.
The voice of the LORD is upon the waters:
    the God of glory thundereth:
    the LORD is upon many waters.

The voice of the LORD is powerful;
  the voice of the LORD is full of majesty.
The voice of the LORD breaketh the cedars; yea,
  the LORD breaketh the cedars of Lebanon.
He maketh them also to skip like a calf;
  Lebanon and Sirion like a young unicorn.
The voice of the LORD divideth
  the flames of fire.
The voice of the LORD shaketh the wilderness;
  the LORD shaketh the wilderness of Kadesh.
The voice of the LORD maketh the hinds to calve,
  and discovereth the forests:
  and in his temple doth every one speak of his glory.
The LORD sitteth upon the flood;
  yea, the LORD sitteth King for ever.
The LORD will give strength unto his people;
  the LORD will bless his people with peace.

Open your ears to hear the Word of the Lord.

A READING FROM SACRED SCRIPTURE
Isaiah 35:1–10 (NCV)

The desert and dry land will become happy;
  the desert will be glad and will produce flowers.
Like a flower, it will have many blooms.
  It will show its happiness, as if it were shouting with joy.
It will be beautiful like the forest of Lebanon,
  as beautiful as the hill of Carmel and the Plain of Sharon.
Everyone will see the glory of the LORD
  and the splendor of our God.
Make the weak hands strong
  and the weak knees steady.
Say to people who are frightened,
  "Be strong. Don't be afraid.
Look, your God will come,
  and he will punish your enemies.

He will make them pay for the wrongs they did,
> but he will save you."
Then the blind people will see again,
> and the deaf will hear.
Crippled people will jump like deer,
> and those who can't talk now will shout with joy.
Water will flow in the desert,
> and streams will flow in the dry land.
The burning desert will have pools of water,
> and the dry ground will have springs.
Where wild dogs once lived,
> grass and water plants will grow.
A road will be there;
> this highway will be called "The Road to Being Holy."
Evil people will not be allowed to walk on that road;
> only good people will walk on it.
> No fools will go on it.
No lions will be there,
> nor will dangerous animals be on that road.
> They will not be found there.
That road will be for the people God saves;
> the people the LORD has freed will return there.
They will enter Jerusalem with joy,
> and their happiness will last forever.
Their gladness and joy will fill them completely,
> and sorrow and sadness will go far away.

The Word of the Lord.
Thanks be to God.

Pray now for your own needs and for the needs of others.

Allot ample time to freely express your prayers.

INTERCESSION

The earth is yours and everything in it,
King of Glory, hear our prayers.
You founded it upon the sea, upon the waters;
King of Glory, hear our prayers.
You clean our hands from the dirt of our sin;
King of Glory, hear our prayers.
You lead us up the mountain, your holy hill;
King of Glory, hear our prayers.
Who is this King of Glory?
The Lord Almighty—he will hear our prayers.

The disciples inquired, "Lord, teach us to pray." We join with his reply.

THE LORD'S PRAYER

Our Father, who art in heaven, hallowed be thy name. Thy Kingdom come, thy will be done, on earth as it is in heaven. Give us this day our daily bread. And forgive us our trespasses, as we forgive those who trespass against us. And lead us not into temptation, but deliver us from evil.

Spend a few moments in silence, meditating on the Lord.

CONCLUDING PRAYER

Glorious Father, may you strengthen us deep within our spirits, through your most Holy Spirit—that Christ may dwell in our hearts through faith, giving us the power to grasp the height and depth and breadth of your unending love. And on this day, may we be filled to the measure of all the fullness of who you are. In the blessed name of your Son, our Lord Jesus Christ, and in the fellowship of the Holy Spirit, amen.

2/23/08

Quiet your heart before the Lord, then proceed as you feel ready.

Give thanks to the LORD,
> And call upon his name.
Make known among the nations
> The great works he has done.

Glory to the Father, and to the Son, and to the Holy Spirit. As it was in the beginning, is now, and will be forever: from unending to unending. Amen.

For the mighty works of God, lift your praises.

PSALM 95:1–7
Venite Exultemus

O come, let us sing unto the LORD:
> let us make a joyful noise to the rock of our salvation.
Let us come before his presence with thanksgiving,
> and make a joyful noise unto him with psalms.
Let us shout to the Rock.
For the LORD is a great God,
> and a great King above all gods.
In his hand are the deep places of the earth:
> the strength of the hills is his also.
The sea is his, and he made it:
> and his hands formed the dry land.
Let us worship our Lord, our Creator.
O come, let us worship and bow down:
> let us kneel before the LORD our maker.

For he is our God;
> and we are the people of his pasture,
> and the sheep of his hand.
> *For he is the Great Shepherd.*

Let us kneel and ask God to cleanse us from all unrighteousness.

PRAYER OF CONFESSION

Most holy and gracious God, we confess to you that we don't always get it right. We don't always love as you have called us to love. We don't often enough answer your invitation to serve. We don't continually seek the lost. But Father, you get it right with us every time. Accept our humble confession, and sanctify us by the power and beauty of your Word, that we may live in the light of your goodness, serve with the warmth of your gentleness, and love with the passion of your grace. Forever and ever, let it be so.

Pause for a moment to reflect on your repentance.

Then join with the psalmist's heart, giving praise and adoration.

PSALM 30:1–5
Exaltabo Te, Domine

I will extol thee, O LORD;
> for thou hast lifted me up,
> and hast not made my foes to rejoice over me.
O LORD my God, I cried unto thee,
> and thou hast healed me.
O LORD, thou hast brought up my soul from the grave:
> thou hast kept me alive, that I should not go down to the pit.
Sing unto the LORD, O ye saints of his,
> and give thanks at the remembrance of his holiness.
For his anger endureth but a moment;
> in his favour is life:
> weeping may endure for a night,
> but joy cometh in the morning.

Open your ears to hear the Word of the Lord.

A READING FROM SACRED SCRIPTURE
Romans 5:1–11 (NIV)

Therefore, since we have been justified through faith, we have peace with God through our Lord Jesus Christ, through whom we have gained access by faith into this grace in which we now stand. And we rejoice in the hope of the glory of God. Not only so, but we also rejoice in our sufferings, because we know that suffering produces perseverance; perseverance, character; and character, hope. And hope does not disappoint us, because God has poured out his love into our hearts by the Holy Spirit, whom he has given us.

You see, at just the right time, when we were still powerless, Christ died for the ungodly. Very rarely will anyone die for a righteous man, though for a good man someone might possibly dare to die. But God demonstrates his own love for us in this: While we were still sinners, Christ died for us.

Since we have now been justified by his blood, how much more shall we be saved from God's wrath through him! For if, when we were God's enemies, we were reconciled to him through the death of his Son, how much more, having been reconciled, shall we be saved through his life! Not only is this so, but we also rejoice in God through our Lord Jesus Christ, through whom we have now received reconciliation.

The Word of the Lord.
Thanks be to God.

Pray now for your own needs and for the needs of others.

Allot ample time to freely express your prayers.

INTERCESSION

Blessed are the poor in spirit,
For theirs is the kingdom of heaven.
Blessed are those who mourn,
For they will be comforted.

Blessed are the meek,
For they will inherit the earth.
Blessed are those who hunger for righteousness,
For they will be filled.
Blessed are the merciful,
For they will be shown mercy.
Blessed are the pure in heart,
For they will see God.
Blessed are the peacemakers,
For they will be called sons of God.

The disciples inquired, "Lord, teach us to pray." We join with his reply.

THE LORD'S PRAYER

Our Father, who art in heaven, hallowed be thy name. Thy Kingdom come, thy will be done, on earth as it is in heaven. Give us this day our daily bread. And forgive us our trespasses, as we forgive those who trespass against us. And lead us not into temptation, but deliver us from evil.

Spend a few moments in silence, meditating on the Lord.

CONCLUDING PRAYER

Glorious Father, may you strengthen us deep within our spirits, through your most Holy Spirit—that Christ may dwell in our hearts through faith, giving us the power to grasp the height and depth and breadth of your unending love. And on this day, may we be filled to the measure of all the fullness of who you are. In the blessed name of your Son, our Lord Jesus Christ, and in the fellowship of the Holy Spirit, amen.

Quiet your heart before the Lord, then proceed as you feel ready.

From the rising of the sun,
    The name of the LORD is to be praised.
To the place where it sets,
    The name of the LORD is to be praised.

Glory to the Father, and to the Son, and to the Holy Spirit. As it was in the beginning, is now, and will be forever: from unending to unending. Amen.

For the mighty works of God, lift your praises.

PSALM 146:1–8
Lauda, Anima Mea

Praise ye the LORD.
    Praise the LORD, O my soul.
While I live will I praise the LORD:
    I will sing praises unto my God while I have any being.
Praise the LORD, O my soul.
Put not your trust in princes,
    nor in the son of man, in whom there is no help.
His breath goeth forth, he returneth to his earth;
    in that very day his thoughts perish.
Praise the LORD, O my soul.
Happy is he that hath the God of Jacob for his help,
    whose hope is in the LORD his God:
Which made heaven, and earth,
    the sea, and all that therein is:

which keepeth truth for ever:
Praise the LORD, O my soul.
Which executeth judgment for the oppressed:
  which giveth food to the hungry.
The LORD looseth the prisoners:
The LORD openeth the eyes of the blind:
  the LORD raiseth them that are bowed down:
  the LORD loveth the righteous:
Praise the LORD, O my soul.

Let us kneel and ask God to cleanse us from all unrighteousness.

PRAYER OF CONFESSION

Most holy and gracious God, we confess to you that we don't always get it right. We don't always love as you have called us to love. We don't often enough answer your invitation to serve. We don't continually seek the lost. But Father, you get it right with us every time. Accept our humble confession, and sanctify us by the power and beauty of your Word, that we may live in the light of your goodness, serve with the warmth of your gentleness, and love with the passion of your grace. Forever and ever, let it be so.

Pause for a moment to reflect on your repentance.

Then join with the psalmist's heart, giving praise and adoration.

PSALM 32:1–5
Beati Quorum

Blessed is he
  whose transgression is forgiven,
  whose sin is covered.
Blessed is the man
  unto whom the LORD imputeth not iniquity,
  and in whose spirit there is no guile.
When I kept silence,
  my bones waxed old

through my roaring all the day long.
For day and night
> thy hand was heavy upon me:
> my moisture is turned
> into the drought of summer.
> Selah.
I acknowledged my sin unto thee,
> and mine iniquity have I not hid.
> I said, I will confess
> my transgressions unto the LORD;
> and thou forgavest
> the iniquity of my sin.
> Selah.

Open your ears to hear the Word of the Lord.

A READING FROM SACRED SCRIPTURE
Isaiah 37:14–20 (NCV)

When Hezekiah received the letter from the messengers and read it, he went up to the Temple of the LORD. He spread the letter out before the LORD and prayed to the LORD: "LORD All-Powerful, you are the God of Israel, whose throne is between the gold creatures with wings, only you are God of all the kingdoms of the earth. You made the heavens and the earth. Hear, LORD, and listen. Open your eyes, LORD, and see. Listen to all the words Sennacherib has said to insult the living God.

"It is true, LORD, that the kings of Assyria have destroyed all these countries and their lands. They have thrown the gods of these nations into the fire, but they were only wood and rock statues that people made. So the kings have destroyed them. Now, LORD our God, save us from the king's power so that all the kingdoms of the earth will know that you, LORD, are the only God."

The Word of the Lord.
Thanks be to God.

Pray now for your own needs and for the needs of others.

Allot ample time to freely express your prayers.

INTERCESSION

Cleanse me with hyssop, and I will be clean;
Wash me, and I will be whiter than snow.
Hide your face from my sins
And blot out all my iniquity.
Create in me a pure heart, O God,
And renew a steadfast spirit within me.
Do not cast me from your presence
Or take your Holy Spirit from me.
Restore to me the joy of your salvation
And grant me a willing spirit, to sustain me.

The disciples inquired, "Lord, teach us to pray." We join with his reply.

THE LORD'S PRAYER

Our Father, who art in heaven, hallowed be thy name. Thy Kingdom come, thy will be done, on earth as it is in heaven. Give us this day our daily bread. And forgive us our trespasses, as we forgive those who trespass against us. And lead us not into temptation, but deliver us from evil.

Spend a few moments in silence, meditating on the Lord.

CONCLUDING PRAYER

Glorious Father, may you strengthen us deep within our spirits, through your most Holy Spirit—that Christ may dwell in our hearts through faith, giving us the power to grasp the height and depth and breadth of your unending love. And on this day, may we be filled to the measure of all the fullness of who you are. In the blessed name of your Son, our Lord Jesus Christ, and in the fellowship of the Holy Spirit, amen.

2/25

Quiet your heart before the Lord, then proceed as you feel ready.

Love the LORD,
    All you his saints.
Love the LORD your God,
    All you his faithful.

Glory to the Father, and to the Son, and to the Holy Spirit. As it was in
the beginning, is now, and will be forever: from unending to unending.
Amen.

For the mighty works of God, lift your praises.

PSALM 67
Deus Misereatur

God be merciful unto us, and bless us;
    and cause his face to shine upon us;
    Selah.
That thy way may be known upon earth,
    thy saving health among all nations.
O God, shine upon us.
Let the people praise thee, O God;
    let all the people praise thee.
O let the nations be glad and sing for joy:
    for thou shalt judge the people righteously,
    and govern the nations upon earth.
    Selah.
Let the people praise thee, O God;

let all the people praise thee.
O God, may we, your people, praise you.
Then shall the earth yield her increase;
    and God, even our own God, shall bless us.
God shall bless us;
    and all the ends of the earth shall fear him.
O God, may we, your people, praise you.

Let us kneel and ask God to cleanse us from all unrighteousness.

PRAYER OF CONFESSION

Most holy and gracious God, we confess to you that we don't always get it right. We don't always love as you have called us to love. We don't often enough answer your invitation to serve. We don't continually seek the lost. But Father, you get it right with us every time. Accept our humble confession, and sanctify us by the power and beauty of your Word, that we may live in the light of your goodness, serve with the warmth of your gentleness, and love with the passion of your grace. Forever and ever, let it be so.

Pause for a moment to reflect on your repentance.

Then join with the psalmist's heart, giving praise and adoration.

PSALM 33:1–9
Exultate, Justi

Rejoice in the LORD, O ye righteous:
    for praise is comely for the upright.
Praise the LORD with harp:
    sing unto him with the psaltery and an instrument of ten
        strings.
Sing unto him a new song;
    play skilfully with a loud noise.
For the word of the LORD is right;
    and all his works are done in truth.
He loveth righteousness and judgment:

the earth is full of the goodness of the LORD.
By the word of the LORD were the heavens made;
    and all the host of them by the breath of his mouth.
He gathereth the waters of the sea together as an heap:
    he layeth up the depth in storehouses.
Let all the earth fear the LORD:
    let all the inhabitants of the world stand in awe of him.
For he spake, and it was done;
    he commanded, and it stood fast.

Open your ears to hear the Word of the Lord.

A READING FROM SACRED SCRIPTURE
Romans 6:8–18 (NIV)

Now if we died with Christ, we believe that we will also live with him. For we know that since Christ was raised from the dead, he cannot die again; death no longer has mastery over him. The death he died, he died to sin once for all; but the life he lives, he lives to God.

In the same way, count yourselves dead to sin but alive to God in Christ Jesus. Therefore do not let sin reign in your mortal body so that you obey its evil desires. Do not offer the parts of your body to sin, as instruments of wickedness, but rather offer yourselves to God, as those who have been brought from death to life; and offer the parts of your body to him as instruments of righteousness. For sin shall not be your master, because you are not under law, but under grace.

What then? Shall we sin because we are not under law but under grace? By no means! Don't you know that when you offer yourselves to someone to obey him as slaves, you are slaves to the one whom you obey—whether you are slaves to sin, which leads to death, or to obedience, which leads to righteousness? But thanks be to God that, though you used to be slaves to sin, you wholeheartedly obeyed the form of teaching to which you were entrusted. You have been set free from sin and have become slaves to righteousness.

The Word of the Lord.
Thanks be to God.

Pray now for your own needs and for the needs of others.

Allot ample time to freely express your prayers.

INTERCESSION

Show us your mercy, O Lord;
  And grant us your salvation.
Clothe your ministers with righteousness;
  Let your people sing with joy.
Give peace, O Lord, in all the world;
  For only in you can we live in safety.
Lord, keep this nation under your care;
  And guide us in the way of justice and truth.
Let your way be known upon earth;
  Your saving health among all nations.
Let not the needy, O Lord, be forgotten;
  Nor the hope of the poor be taken away.
Create in us clean hearts, O God;
  And sustain us with your Holy Spirit.

The disciples inquired, "Lord, teach us to pray." We join with his reply.

THE LORD'S PRAYER

Our Father, who art in heaven, hallowed be thy name. Thy Kingdom come, thy will be done, on earth as it is in heaven. Give us this day our daily bread. And forgive us our trespasses, as we forgive those who trespass against us. And lead us not into temptation, but deliver us from evil.

Spend a few moments in silence, meditating on the Lord.

CONCLUDING PRAYER

Glorious Father, may you strengthen us deep within our spirits, through your most Holy Spirit—that Christ may dwell in our hearts through faith, giving us the power to grasp the height and depth and breadth of your unending love. And on this day, may we be filled to the measure of all the fullness of who you are. In the blessed name of your Son, our Lord Jesus Christ, and in the fellowship of the Holy Spirit, amen.

Quiet your heart before the Lord, then proceed as you feel ready.

Ascribe to the LORD
>The glory due his name.
Worship the LORD
>In the splendor of his holiness.

Glory to the Father, and to the Son, and to the Holy Spirit. As it was in the beginning, is now, and will be forever: from unending to unending. Amen.

For the mighty works of God, lift your praises.

PSALM 148:1–12
Laudate Dominum

Praise ye the LORD.
>Praise ye the LORD from the heavens:
>praise him in the heights.
Praise ye him, all his angels:
>praise ye him, all his hosts.
Let us praise the LORD.
Praise ye him, sun and moon:

praise him, all ye stars of light.
Praise him, ye heavens of heavens,
    and ye waters that be above the heavens.
Let them praise the name of the LORD:
    for he commanded, and they were created.
He hath also stablished them for ever and ever:
    he hath made a decree which shall not pass.
Let them praise the LORD.
Praise the LORD from the earth,
    ye dragons, and all deeps:
Fire, and hail; snow, and vapour;
    stormy wind fulfilling his word:
Mountains, and all hills;
    fruitful trees, and all cedars:
Beasts, and all cattle;
    creeping things, and flying fowl:
Kings of the earth, and all people;
    princes, and all judges of the earth:
Both young men, and maidens;
    old men, and children:
Let all voices praise the LORD.

Let us kneel and ask God to cleanse us from all unrighteousness.

PRAYER OF CONFESSION

Most holy and gracious God, we confess to you that we don't always get it right. We don't always love as you have called us to love. We don't often enough answer your invitation to serve. We don't continually seek the lost. But Father, you get it right with us every time. Accept our humble confession, and sanctify us by the power and beauty of your Word, that we may live in the light of your goodness, serve with the warmth of your gentleness, and love with the passion of your grace. Forever and ever, let it be so.

Pause for a moment to reflect on your repentance.

Then join with the psalmist's heart, giving praise and adoration.

PSALM 90
Domine, Refugium

LORD, thou hast been our dwelling place
    in all generations.
Before the mountains were brought forth
    or ever thou hadst formed the earth and the world,
    even from everlasting to everlasting, thou art God.
Thou turnest man to destruction;
    and sayest, Return, ye children of men.
For a thousand years in thy sight
    are but as yesterday when it is past,
    and as a watch in the night.
Thou carriest them away as with a flood; they are as a sleep:
    in the morning they are like grass which groweth up.
In the morning it flourisheth, and groweth up;
    in the evening it is cut down, and withereth.
For we are consumed by thine anger,
    and by thy wrath are we troubled.
Thou hast set our iniquities before thee,
    our secret sins in the light of thy countenance.
For all our days are passed away in thy wrath:
    we spend our years as a tale that is told.
The days of our years are threescore years and ten;
    and if by reason of strength they be fourscore years,
    yet is their strength labour and sorrow;
    for it is soon cut off, and we fly away.
Who knoweth the power of thine anger?
    even according to thy fear, so is thy wrath.
So teach us to number our days,
    that we may apply our hearts unto wisdom.
Return, O LORD, how long?
    and let it repent thee concerning thy servants.
O satisfy us early with thy mercy;
    that we may rejoice and be glad all our days.

Make us glad according to the days wherein thou hast afflicted us,
and the years wherein we have seen evil.
Let thy work appear unto thy servants,
and thy glory unto their children.
And let the beauty of the LORD our God be upon us:
and establish thou the work of our hands upon us;
yea, the work of our hands establish thou it.

Open your ears to hear the Word of the Lord.

A READING FROM SACRED SCRIPTURE
Isaiah 40:1–11 (NCV)

Your God says,
"Comfort, comfort my people.
Speak kindly to the people of Jerusalem
and tell them
that their time of service is finished,
that they have paid for their sins,
that the LORD has punished Jerusalem
twice for every sin they did."
This is the voice of one who calls out:
"Prepare in the desert
the way for the LORD.
Make a straight road in the dry lands
for our God.
Every valley should be raised up,
and every mountain and hill should be made flat.
The rough ground should be made level,
and the rugged ground should be made smooth.
Then the glory of the LORD will be shown,
and all people together will see it.
The LORD himself said these things."
A voice says, "Cry out!"
Then I said, "What shall I cry out?"
"Say all people are like the grass,
and all their glory is like the flowers of the field.

The grass dies and the flowers fall
>   when the breath of the LORD blows on them.
>   Surely the people are like grass.
The grass dies and the flowers fall,
>   but the word of our God will live forever."
Jerusalem, you have good news to tell.
>   Go up on a high mountain.
Jerusalem, you have good news to tell.
>   Shout out loud the good news.
Shout it out and don't be afraid.
>   Say to the towns of Judah,
>   "Here is your God."
Look, the Lord GOD is coming with power
>   to rule all the people.
Look, he will bring reward for his people;
>   he will have their payment with him.
He takes care of his people like a shepherd.
>   He gathers them like lambs in his arms
>   and carries them close to him.
He gently leads the mothers of the lambs.

The Word of the Lord.
Thanks be to God.

Pray now for your own needs and for the needs of others.
Allot ample time to freely express your prayers.

INTERCESSION

How wonderful are you, our God;
>   *How infinite is your wisdom.*
You cover us with arms of grace;
>   *You protect us, your children.*
Great, are your ways, O Lord;
>   *Great, your unending love for us.*
Forever we will offer you
>   *All of our praise.*

For you are full of compassion
And show mercy to your servants.

The disciples inquired, "Lord, teach us to pray." We join with his reply.

THE LORD'S PRAYER

Our Father, who art in heaven, hallowed be thy name. Thy Kingdom come, thy will be done, on earth as it is in heaven. Give us this day our daily bread. And forgive us our trespasses, as we forgive those who trespass against us. And lead us not into temptation, but deliver us from evil.

Spend a few moments in silence, meditating on the Lord.

CONCLUDING PRAYER

Glorious Father, may you strengthen us deep within our spirits, through your most Holy Spirit—that Christ may dwell in our hearts through faith, giving us the power to grasp the height and depth and breadth of your unending love. And on this day, may we be filled to the measure of all the fullness of who you are. In the blessed name of your Son, our Lord Jesus Christ, and in the fellowship of the Holy Spirit, amen.

2/27

Quiet your heart before the Lord, then proceed as you feel ready.

LORD, open our lips,
>And our mouths shall proclaim your praise.

Gloria Patri

Glory to the Father, and to the Son, and to the Holy Spirit. As it was in the beginning, is now, and will be forever: from unending to unending. Amen.

For the mighty works of God, lift your praises.

PSALM 100
Jubilate Deo

Make a joyful noise unto the LORD, all ye lands.
Serve the LORD with gladness:
>come before his presence with singing.

Be joyful in the LORD, all you lands.
Know ye that the LORD he is God:
>it is he that hath made us, and not we ourselves;
>we are his people, and the sheep of his pasture.

Be joyful in the LORD, all you lands.
Enter into his gates with thanksgiving,
>and into his courts with praise:
>be thankful unto him, and bless his name.

Be joyful in the LORD, all you lands.
For the LORD is good; his mercy is everlasting;
>and his truth endureth to all generations.

His love and mercy endure forever.

Let us kneel and ask God to cleanse us from all unrighteousness.

PRAYER OF CONFESSION

Most holy and gracious God, we confess to you that we don't always get it right. We don't always love as you have called us to love. We don't often enough answer your invitation to serve. We don't continually seek the lost. But Father, you get it right with us every time. Accept our humble confession, and sanctify us by the power and beauty of your Word, that we may live in the light of your goodness, serve with the warmth of your gentleness, and love with the passion of your grace. Forever and ever, let it be so.

Pause for a moment to reflect on your repentance.

Then join with the psalmist's heart, giving praise and adoration.

PSALM 91
Qui Habitat

He that dwelleth in the secret place of the most High
    shall abide under the shadow of the Almighty.
I will say of the LORD, He is my refuge and my fortress:
    my God; in him will I trust.
Surely he shall deliver thee from the snare of the fowler,
    and from the noisome pestilence.
He shall cover thee with his feathers,
    and under his wings shalt thou trust:
    his truth shall be thy shield and buckler.
Thou shalt not be afraid for the terror by night;
    nor for the arrow that flieth by day;
Nor for the pestilence that walketh in darkness;
    nor for the destruction that wasteth at noonday.
A thousand shall fall at thy side,
    and ten thousand at thy right hand;
    but it shall not come nigh thee.
Only with thine eyes shalt thou behold
    and see the reward of the wicked.

Because thou hast made the LORD, which is my refuge,
> even the most High, thy habitation;

There shall no evil befall thee,
> neither shall any plague come nigh thy dwelling.

For he shall give his angels charge over thee,
> to keep thee in all thy ways.

They shall bear thee up in their hands,
> lest thou dash thy foot against a stone.

Thou shalt tread upon the lion and adder:
> the young lion and the dragon shalt thou trample under feet.

Because he hath set his love upon me, therefore will I deliver him:
> I will set him on high, because he hath known my name.

He shall call upon me, and I will answer him:
> I will be with him in trouble;
> I will deliver him, and honour him.

With long life will I satisfy him,
> and shew him my salvation.

Open your ears to hear the Word of the Lord.

A READING FROM SACRED SCRIPTURE
Ephesians 4:1–13 (The Message)

In light of all this, here's what I want you to do. While I'm locked up here, a prisoner for the Master, I want you to get out there and walk—better yet, run!—on the road God called you to travel. I don't want any of you sitting around on your hands. I don't want anyone strolling off, down some path that goes nowhere. And mark that you do this with humility and discipline—not in fits and starts, but steadily, pouring yourselves out for each other in acts of love, alert at noticing differences and quick at mending fences.

You were all called to travel on the same road and in the same direction, so stay together, both outwardly and inwardly. You have one Master, one faith, one baptism, one God and Father of all, who rules over all, works through all, and is present in all. Everything you are and think and do is permeated with Oneness.

But that doesn't mean you should all look and speak and act the same. Out of the generosity of Christ, each of us is given his own gift. The text for this is,

> He climbed the high mountain,
> He captured the enemy and seized the booty,
> He handed it all out in gifts to the people.

It's true, is it not, that the One who climbed up also climbed down, down to the valley of earth? And the One who climbed down is the One who climbed back up, up to highest heaven. He handed out gifts above and below, filled heaven with his gifts, filled earth with his gifts. He handed out gifts of apostle, prophet, evangelist, and pastor-teacher to train Christ's followers in skilled servant work, working within Christ's body, the church, until we're all moving rhythmically and easily with each other, efficient and graceful in response to God's Son, fully mature adults, fully developed within and without, fully alive like Christ.

> *The Word of the Lord.*
> *Thanks be to God.*

Pray now for your own needs and for the needs of others.

Allot ample time to freely express your prayers.

INTERCESSION

Save your people, Lord, and bless your inheritance;
> *Govern and uphold them, now and always.*
Day by day we bless you;
> *We praise your name forever.*
Lord, keep us from all sin today;
> *Have mercy on us, Lord, have mercy.*
Lord, show us your love and mercy;
> *For we put our trust in you.*
In you, Lord, is our hope;
> *And we shall never hope in vain.*

The disciples inquired, "Lord, teach us to pray." We join with his reply.

THE LORD'S PRAYER

Our Father, who art in heaven, hallowed be thy name. Thy Kingdom come, thy will be done, on earth as it is in heaven. Give us this day our daily bread. And forgive us our trespasses, as we forgive those who trespass against us. And lead us not into temptation, but deliver us from evil.

Spend a few moments in silence, meditating on the Lord.

CONCLUDING PRAYER

Most Holy God, you have baptized all who believe in you with the same Spirit, into the same body, of which your Son, Jesus Christ, is the head. Grant us now the unity that you desire, so that we all may be one body, in one spirit. In the blessed name of your Son, our Lord Jesus Christ, and in the fellowship of the Holy Spirit, amen.

DAY TWENTY-THREE

Quiet your heart before the Lord, then proceed as you feel ready.

May the words of our mouths
　　And the meditations of our hearts
Be pleasing in your sight,
　　O LORD, our Rock and our Redeemer.

Glory to the Father, and to the Son, and to the Holy Spirit. As it was in the beginning, is now, and will be forever: from unending to unending. Amen.

For the mighty works of God, lift your praises.

PSALM 147:1-9
Laudate Dominum

Praise ye the LORD:
>for it is good to sing praises unto our God;
>for it is pleasant; and praise is comely.

It is good to praise the LORD.
The LORD doth build up Jerusalem:
>he gathereth together the outcasts of Israel.

He healeth the broken in heart,
>and bindeth up their wounds.

The LORD is worthy of praise.
He telleth the number of the stars;
>he calleth them all by their names.

Great is our Lord, and of great power:
>his understanding is infinite.

The LORD lifteth up the meek:
>he casteth the wicked down to the ground.

Our God is great and mighty.
Sing unto the LORD with thanksgiving;
>sing praise upon the harp unto our God:

Who covereth the heaven with clouds,
>who prepareth rain for the earth,
>who maketh grass to grow upon the mountains.

He giveth to the beast his food,
>and to the young ravens which cry.

Sing to the LORD who provides.

Let us kneel and ask God to cleanse us from all unrighteousness.

PRAYER OF CONFESSION

Most holy and gracious God, we confess to you that we don't always get it right. We don't always love as you have called us to love. We don't often enough answer your invitation to serve. We don't continually seek the lost. But Father, you get it right with us every time. Accept our humble confession, and sanctify us by the power and beauty of your Word, that we may live in the light of your goodness, serve with the warmth of your gentleness, and love with the passion of your grace. Forever and ever, let it be so.

Pause for a moment to reflect on your repentance.

Then join with the psalmist's heart, giving praise and adoration.

PSALM 92:1–8
Bonum Est Confiteri

It is a good thing to give thanks unto the LORD,
    And to sing praises unto thy name, O most High:
To shew forth thy lovingkindness in the morning,
    and thy faithfulness every night,
Upon an instrument of ten strings, and upon the psaltery;
    upon the harp with a solemn sound.
For thou, LORD, hast made me glad through thy work:
    I will triumph in the works of thy hands.
O LORD, how great are thy works!
    and thy thoughts are very deep.
A brutish man knoweth not;
    neither doth a fool understand this.
When the wicked spring as the grass,
    and when all the workers of iniquity do flourish;
    it is that they shall be destroyed for ever:
But thou, LORD, art most high for evermore.

Open your ears to hear the Word of the Lord.

A READING FROM SACRED SCRIPTURE
Isaiah 42:5–13 (NCV)

God, the LORD, said these things.
He created the skies and stretched them out.
    He spread out the earth and everything on it.
He gives life to all people on earth,
    to everyone who walks on the earth.
The LORD says, "I, the LORD, called you to do right,
    and I will hold your hand
and protect you.
    You will be the sign of my agreement with the people,
    a light to shine for all people.
You will help the blind to see.
    You will free those who are in prison,
    and you will lead those who live in darkness out of their
        prison.
"I am the LORD. That is my name.
    I will not give my glory to another;
    I will not let idols take the praise that should be mine.
The things I said would happen have happened,
    and now I tell you about new things.
Before those things happen,
    I tell you about them."
Sing a new song to the LORD;
    sing his praise everywhere on the earth.
Praise him, you people who sail on the seas and you animals
        who live in them.
    Praise him, you people living in faraway places.
The deserts and their cities should praise him.
    The settlements of Kedar should praise him.
The people living in Sela should sing for joy;
    they should shout from the mountaintops.
They should give glory to the LORD.
    People in faraway lands should praise him.
The LORD will march out like a strong soldier;
    he will be excited like a man ready to fight a war.

He will shout out the battle cry
and defeat his enemies.

The Word of the Lord.
Thanks be to God.

Pray now for your own needs and for the needs of others.

Allot ample time to freely express your prayers.

INTERCESSION

We will exalt your name, O Lord,
For you have heard our cries,
And you have healed us.
The Lord has lifted us up from the depths.
We will sing praises to you our Lord,
For your anger is fleeting,
But your favor lasts forever.
The Lord has lifted us up from the depths.
Our hearts cannot stay silent,
Forever we will give you thanks.
The Lord has lifted us up from the depths.

The disciples inquired, "Lord, teach us to pray." We join with his reply.

THE LORD'S PRAYER

Our Father, who art in heaven, hallowed be thy name. Thy Kingdom
come, thy will be done, on earth as it is in heaven. Give us this day
our daily bread. And forgive us our trespasses, as we forgive those
who trespass against us. And lead us not into temptation, but deliver
us from evil.

Spend a few moments in silence, meditating on the Lord.

CONCLUDING PRAYER

Most Holy God, you have baptized all who believe in you with the same Spirit, into the same body, of which your Son, Jesus Christ, is the head. Grant us now the unity that you desire, so that we all may be one body, in one spirit. In the blessed name of your Son, our Lord Jesus Christ, and in the fellowship of the Holy Spirit, amen.

Quiet your heart before the Lord, then proceed as you feel ready.

Teach us your way, O LORD,
 And we will walk in your truth.
Give us undivided hearts,
 That we may fear your name.

Glory to the Father, and to the Son, and to the Holy Spirit. As it was in the beginning, is now, and will be forever: from unending to unending. Amen.

For the mighty works of God, lift your praises.

PSALM 149:1–4
Cantate Domino

 Praise ye the LORD.
  Sing unto the LORD a new song,
  and his praise in the congregation of saints.

Sing to the LORD a new song.
Let Israel rejoice in him that made him:
> let the children of Zion be joyful in their King.

Let them praise his name in the dance:
> let them sing praises unto him with the timbrel and harp.

Make music for the LORD our God.
For the LORD taketh pleasure in his people:
> he will beautify the meek with salvation.

For the LORD saves us.

Let us kneel and ask God to cleanse us from all unrighteousness.

PRAYER OF CONFESSION

Most holy and gracious God, we confess to you that we don't always get it right. We don't always love as you have called us to love. We don't often enough answer your invitation to serve. We don't continually seek the lost. But Father, you get it right with us every time. Accept our humble confession, and sanctify us by the power and beauty of your Word, that we may live in the light of your goodness, serve with the warmth of your gentleness, and love with the passion of your grace. Forever and ever, let it be so.

Pause for a moment to reflect on your repentance.

Then join with the psalmist's heart, giving praise and adoration.

PSALM 93
Dominus Regnavit

The LORD reigneth, he is clothed with majesty;
> the LORD is clothed with strength,
> wherewith he hath girded himself:
> the world also is stablished,
> that it cannot be moved.

Thy throne is established of old:
> thou art from everlasting.

The floods have lifted up, O LORD,

the floods have lifted up their voice;
the floods lift up their waves.
The LORD on high is mightier than the noise of many waters,
yea, than the mighty waves of the sea.
Thy testimonies are very sure:
holiness becometh thine house,
O LORD, for ever.

Open your ears to hear the Word of the Lord.

A READING FROM SACRED SCRIPTURE
Isaiah 43:8–19 (NCV)

Bring out the people who have eyes but don't see
and those who have ears but don't hear.
All the nations gather together,
and all the people come together.
Which of their gods said this would happen?
Which of their gods can tell what happened in the beginning?
Let them bring their witnesses to prove they were right.
Then others will say, "It is true."
The LORD says, "You are my witnesses
and the servant I chose.
I chose you so you would know and believe me,
so you would understand that I am the true God.
There was no God before me,
and there will be no God after me.
I myself am the LORD;
I am the only Savior.
I myself have spoken to you, saved you, and told you these
things.
It was not some foreign god among you.
You are my witnesses, and I am God,"
says the LORD.
"I have always been God.
No one can save people from my power;
when I do something, no one can change it."

This is what the LORD, who saves you,
    the Holy One of Israel, says:
"I will send armies to Babylon for you,
    and I will knock down all its locked gates.
The Babylonians will shout their cries of sorrow.
I am the LORD, your Holy One,
    the Creator of Israel, your King."
This is what the LORD says.
    He is the one who made a road through the sea
    and a path through rough waters.
He is the one who defeated the chariots and horses
    and the mighty armies.
They fell together and will never rise again.
    They were destroyed as a flame is put out.
The LORD says, "Forget what happened before,
    and do not think about the past.
Look at the new thing I am going to do.
    It is already happening. Don't you see it?
I will make a road in the desert
    and rivers in the dry land."

The Word of the Lord.
Thanks be to God.

Pray now for your own needs and for the needs of others.
Allot ample time to freely express your prayers.

INTERCESSION

The earth is yours and everything in it,
    King of Glory, hear our prayers.
You founded it upon the sea, upon the waters;
    King of Glory, hear our prayers.
You clean our hands from the dirt of our sin;
    King of Glory, hear our prayers.
You lead us up the mountain, your holy hill;
    King of Glory, hear our prayers.

Who is this King of Glory?
The Lord Almighty—he will hear our prayers.

The disciples inquired, "Lord, teach us to pray." We join with his reply.

THE LORD'S PRAYER

Our Father, who art in heaven, hallowed be thy name. Thy Kingdom come, thy will be done, on earth as it is in heaven. Give us this day our daily bread. And forgive us our trespasses, as we forgive those who trespass against us. And lead us not into temptation, but deliver us from evil.

Spend a few moments in silence, meditating on the Lord.

CONCLUDING PRAYER

Most Holy God, you have baptized all who believe in you with the same Spirit, into the same body, of which your Son, Jesus Christ, is the head. Grant us now the unity that you desire, so that we all may be one body, in one spirit. In the blessed name of your Son, our Lord Jesus Christ, and in the fellowship of the Holy Spirit, amen.

Quiet your heart before the Lord, then proceed as you feel ready.

Give thanks to the LORD,
    And call upon his name.
Make known among the nations
    The great works he has done.

Glory to the Father, and to the Son, and to the Holy Spirit. As it was in the beginning, is now, and will be forever: from unending to unending. Amen.

For the mighty works of God, lift your praises.

PSALM 95:1–7
Venite Exultemus

O come, let us sing unto the LORD:
    let us make a joyful noise to the rock of our salvation.
Let us come before his presence with thanksgiving,
    and make a joyful noise unto him with psalms.
Let us shout to the Rock.
For the LORD is a great God,
    and a great King above all gods.
In his hand are the deep places of the earth:
    the strength of the hills is his also.
The sea is his, and he made it:
    and his hands formed the dry land.
Let us worship our Lord, our Creator.
O come, let us worship and bow down:

let us kneel before the LORD our maker.
For he is our God;
    and we are the people of his pasture,
    and the sheep of his hand.
For he is the Great Shepherd.

Let us kneel and ask God to cleanse us from all unrighteousness.

PRAYER OF CONFESSION

Most holy and gracious God, we confess to you that we don't always get it right. We don't always love as you have called us to love. We don't often enough answer your invitation to serve. We don't continually seek the lost. But Father, you get it right with us every time. Accept our humble confession, and sanctify us by the power and beauty of your Word, that we may live in the light of your goodness, serve with the warmth of your gentleness, and love with the passion of your grace. Forever and ever, let it be so.

Pause for a moment to reflect on your repentance.

Then join with the psalmist's heart, giving praise and adoration.

PSALM 94:1–11
Deus Ultionum

O LORD God, to whom vengeance belongeth;
    O God, to whom vengeance belongeth, shew thyself.
Lift up thyself, thou judge of the earth:
    render a reward to the proud.
LORD, how long shall the wicked,
    how long shall the wicked triumph?
How long shall they utter and speak hard things?
    and all the workers of iniquity boast themselves?
They break in pieces thy people, O LORD,
    and afflict thine heritage.
They slay the widow and the stranger,
    and murder the fatherless.

Yet they say, The LORD shall not see,
  neither shall the God of Jacob regard it.
Understand, ye brutish among the people:
  and ye fools, when will ye be wise?
He that planted the ear, shall he not hear?
  he that formed the eye, shall he not see?
He that chastiseth the heathen, shall not he correct?
  he that teacheth man knowledge, shall not he know?
The LORD knoweth the thoughts of man,
  that they are vanity.

Open your ears to hear the Word of the Lord.

A READING FROM SACRED SCRIPTURE
Romans 7:11–25 (NIV)

For sin, seizing the opportunity afforded by the commandment, deceived me, and through the commandment put me to death. So then, the law is holy, and the commandment is holy, righteous and good. Did that which is good, then, become death to me? By no means! But in order that sin might be recognized as sin, it produced death in me through what was good, so that through the commandment sin might become utterly sinful.

We know that the law is spiritual; but I am unspiritual, sold as a slave to sin. I do not understand what I do. For what I want to do I do not do, but what I hate I do. And if I do what I do not want to do, I agree that the law is good. As it is, it is no longer I myself who do it, but it is sin living in me. I know that nothing good lives in me, that is, in my sinful nature. For I have the desire to do what is good, but I cannot carry it out. For what I do is not the good I want to do; no, the evil I do not want to do—this I keep on doing. Now if I do what I do not want to do, it is no longer I who do it, but it is sin living in me that does it.

So I find this law at work: When I want to do good, evil is right there with me. For in my inner being I delight in God's law; but I see another law at work in the members of my body, waging war against the law of my mind and making me a prisoner of the law of sin at work within my members. What a wretched man I am! Who

will rescue me from this body of death? Thanks be to God—
through Jesus Christ our Lord!

So then, I myself in my mind am a slave to God's law, but in
the sinful nature a slave to the law of sin.

> *The Word of the Lord.*
> *Thanks be to God.*

Pray now for your own needs and for the needs of others.

Allot ample time to freely express your prayers.

INTERCESSION

Blessed are the poor in spirit,
> *For theirs is the kingdom of heaven.*
Blessed are those who mourn,
> *For they will be comforted.*
Blessed are the meek,
> *For they will inherit the earth.*
Blessed are those who hunger for righteousness,
> *For they will be filled.*
Blessed are the merciful,
> *For they will be shown mercy.*
Blessed are the pure in heart,
> *For they will see God.*
Blessed are the peacemakers,
> *For they will be called sons of God.*

The disciples inquired, "Lord, teach us to pray." We join with his reply.

THE LORD'S PRAYER

Our Father, who art in heaven, hallowed be thy name. Thy Kingdom
come, thy will be done, on earth as it is in heaven. Give us this day
our daily bread. And forgive us our trespasses, as we forgive those
who trespass against us. And lead us not into temptation, but deliver
us from evil.

Spend a few moments in silence, meditating on the Lord.

CONCLUDING PRAYER

Most Holy God, you have baptized all who believe in you with the same Spirit, into the same body, of which your Son, Jesus Christ, is the head. Grant us now the unity that you desire, so that we all may be one body, in one spirit. In the blessed name of your Son, our Lord Jesus Christ, and in the fellowship of the Holy Spirit, amen.

3|4

DAY TWENTY-SIX

DAY TWENTY-SIX

Quiet your heart before the Lord, then proceed as you feel ready.

From the rising of the sun,
    The name of the LORD is to be praised.
To the place where it sets,
    The name of the LORD is to be praised.

Glory to the Father, and to the Son, and to the Holy Spirit. As it was in the beginning, is now, and will be forever: from unending to unending. Amen.

For the mighty works of God, lift your praises.

PSALM 146:1–8

Lauda, Anima Mea

Praise ye the LORD.
    Praise the LORD, O my soul.
While I live will I praise the LORD:
    I will sing praises unto my God while I have any being.
Praise the LORD, O my soul.
Put not your trust in princes,
    nor in the son of man, in whom there is no help.
His breath goeth forth, he returneth to his earth;
    in that very day his thoughts perish.
Praise the LORD, O my soul.
Happy is he that hath the God of Jacob for his help,
    whose hope is in the LORD his God:
Which made heaven, and earth,
    the sea, and all that therein is:
    which keepeth truth for ever:
Praise the LORD, O my soul.
Which executeth judgment for the oppressed:
    which giveth food to the hungry.
The LORD looseth the prisoners:
The LORD openeth the eyes of the blind:
    the LORD raiseth them that are bowed down:
    the LORD loveth the righteous:
Praise the LORD, O my soul.

Let us kneel and ask God to cleanse us from all unrighteousness.

PRAYER OF CONFESSION

Most holy and gracious God, we confess to you that we don't always get it right. We don't always love as you have called us to love. We don't often enough answer your invitation to serve. We don't continually seek the lost. But Father, you get it right with us every time. Accept our humble confession, and sanctify us by the power and beauty of your Word, that we may live in the light of your goodness, serve with the warmth of your gentleness, and love with the passion of your grace. Forever and ever, let it be so.

Pause for a moment to reflect on your repentance.

Then join with the psalmist's heart, giving praise and adoration.

PSALM 96:1–9
Cantate Domino

O sing unto the LORD a new song:
    sing unto the LORD, all the earth.
Sing unto the LORD, bless his name;
    shew forth his salvation from day to day.
Declare his glory among the heathen,
    his wonders among all people.
For the LORD is great, and greatly to be praised:
    he is to be feared above all gods.
For all the gods of the nations are idols:
    but the LORD made the heavens.
Honour and majesty are before him:
    strength and beauty are in his sanctuary.
Give unto the LORD, O ye kindreds of the people,
    give unto the LORD glory and strength.
Give unto the LORD the glory due unto his name:
    bring an offering, and come into his courts.
O worship the LORD in the beauty of holiness:
    fear before him, all the earth.

Open your ears to hear the Word of the Lord.

A READING FROM SACRED SCRIPTURE
Isaiah 44:1–8 (NCV)

The LORD says, "People of Jacob, you are my servants. Listen
    to me!
    People of Israel, I chose you."
This is what the LORD says, who made you,

who formed you in your mother's body,
who will help you:
"People of Jacob, my servants, don't be afraid.
Israel, I chose you.
I will pour out water for the thirsty land
and make streams flow on dry land.
I will pour out my Spirit into your children
and my blessing on your descendants.
Your children will grow like a tree in the grass,
like poplar trees growing beside streams of water.
One person will say, 'I belong to the LORD,'
and another will use the name Jacob.
Another will sign his name 'I am the LORD's,'
and another will use the name Israel."
The LORD, the king of Israel,
is the LORD All-Powerful, who saves Israel.
This is what he says: "I am the beginning and the end.
I am the only God.
Who is a god like me?
That god should come and prove it.
Let him tell and explain all that has happened since I set up my
ancient people.
He should also tell what will happen in the future.
Don't be afraid! Don't worry!
I have always told you what will happen.
You are my witnesses.
There is no other God but me.
I know of no other Rock; I am the only One."

The Word of the Lord.
Thanks be to God.

Pray now for your own needs and for the needs of others.

Allot ample time to freely express your prayers.

INTERCESSION

Cleanse me with hyssop, and I will be clean;
Wash me, and I will be whiter than snow.
Hide your face from my sins
And blot out all my iniquity.
Create in me a pure heart, O God,
And renew a steadfast spirit within me.
Do not cast me from your presence
Or take your Holy Spirit from me.
Restore to me the joy of your salvation
And grant me a willing spirit, to sustain me.

The disciples inquired, "Lord, teach us to pray." We join with his reply.

THE LORD'S PRAYER

Our Father, who art in heaven, hallowed be thy name. Thy Kingdom come, thy will be done, on earth as it is in heaven. Give us this day our daily bread. And forgive us our trespasses, as we forgive those who trespass against us. And lead us not into temptation, but deliver us from evil.

Spend a few moments in silence, meditating on the Lord.

CONCLUDING PRAYER

Most Holy God, you have baptized all who believe in you with the same Spirit, into the same body, of which your Son, Jesus Christ, is the head. Grant us now the unity that you desire, so that we all may be one body, in one spirit. In the blessed name of your Son, our Lord Jesus Christ, and in the fellowship of the Holy Spirit, amen.

DAY TWENTY-SEVEN

Quiet your heart before the Lord, then proceed as you feel ready.

Love the LORD,
    All you his saints.
Love the LORD your God,
    All you his faithful.

Glory to the Father, and to the Son, and to the Holy Spirit. As it was in
the beginning, is now, and will be forever: from unending to unending.
Amen.

For the mighty works of God, lift your praises.

PSALM 67
Deus Misereatur

God be merciful unto us, and bless us;
    and cause his face to shine upon us;
    Selah.
That thy way may be known upon earth,
    thy saving health among all nations.
O God, shine upon us.
Let the people praise thee, O God;
    let all the people praise thee.
O let the nations be glad and sing for joy:
    for thou shalt judge the people righteously,
    and govern the nations upon earth.
    Selah.
Let the people praise thee, O God;

let all the people praise thee.
O God, may we, your people, praise you.
Then shall the earth yield her increase;
   and God, even our own God, shall bless us.
God shall bless us;
   and all the ends of the earth shall fear him.
O God, may we, your people, praise you.

Let us kneel and ask God to cleanse us from all unrighteousness.

PRAYER OF CONFESSION

Most holy and gracious God, we confess to you that we don't always get it right. We don't always love as you have called us to love. We don't often enough answer your invitation to serve. We don't continually seek the lost. But Father, you get it right with us every time. Accept our humble confession, and sanctify us by the power and beauty of your Word, that we may live in the light of your goodness, serve with the warmth of your gentleness, and love with the passion of your grace. Forever and ever, let it be so.

Pause for a moment to reflect on your repentance.

Then join with the psalmist's heart, giving praise and adoration.

PSALM 97
Dominus Regnavit

The LORD reigneth; let the earth rejoice;
   let the multitude of isles be glad thereof.
Clouds and darkness are round about him:
      righteousness and judgment are the habitation of his
         throne.
A fire goeth before him,
   and burneth up his enemies round about.
His lightnings enlightened the world:
   the earth saw, and trembled.
The hills melted like wax at the presence of the LORD,

at the presence of the Lord of the whole earth.
The heavens declare his righteousness,
and all the people see his glory.
Confounded be all they that serve graven images,
that boast themselves of idols:
worship him, all ye gods.
Zion heard, and was glad;
and the daughters of Judah rejoiced
because of thy judgments, O LORD.
For thou, LORD, art high above all the earth:
thou art exalted far above all gods.
Ye that love the LORD, hate evil:
he preserveth the souls of his saints;
he delivereth them out of the hand of the wicked.
Light is sown for the righteous,
and gladness for the upright in heart.
Rejoice in the LORD, ye righteous;
and give thanks at the remembrance of his holiness.

Open your ears to hear the Word of the Lord.

A READING FROM SACRED SCRIPTURE
Romans 8:1–17 (NIV)

Therefore, there is now no condemnation for those who are in Christ Jesus, because through Christ Jesus the law of the Spirit of life set me free from the law of sin and death. For what the law was powerless to do in that it was weakened by the sinful nature, God did by sending his own Son in the likeness of sinful man to be a sin offering. And so he condemned sin in sinful man, in order that the righteous requirements of the law might be fully met in us, who do not live according to the sinful nature but according to the Spirit.

Those who live according to the sinful nature have their minds set on what that nature desires; but those who live in accordance with the Spirit have their minds set on what the Spirit desires. The mind of sinful man is death, but the mind controlled by the Spirit is life and peace; the sinful mind is hostile to God. It does not submit to God's law, nor can it do so. Those controlled by the sinful nature cannot please God.

You, however, are controlled not by the sinful nature but by the Spirit, if the Spirit of God lives in you. And if anyone does not have the Spirit of Christ, he does not belong to Christ. But if Christ is in you, your body is dead because of sin, yet your spirit is alive because of righteousness. And if the Spirit of him who raised Jesus from the dead is living in you, he who raised Christ from the dead will also give life to your mortal bodies through his Spirit, who lives in you.

Therefore, brothers, we have an obligation—but it is not to the sinful nature, to live according to it. For if you live according to the sinful nature, you will die; but if by the Spirit you put to death the misdeeds of the body, you will live, because those who are led by the Spirit of God are sons of God. For you did not receive a spirit that makes you a slave again to fear, but you received the Spirit of sonship. And by him we cry, "Abba, Father." The Spirit himself testifies with our spirit that we are God's children. Now if we are children, then we are heirs—heirs of God and co-heirs with Christ, if indeed we share in his sufferings in order that we may also share in his glory.

The Word of the Lord.
Thanks be to God.

Pray now for your own needs and for the needs of others.

Allot ample time to freely express your prayers.

INTERCESSION

Show us your mercy, O Lord;
And grant us your salvation.
Clothe your ministers with righteousness;
Let your people sing with joy.
Give peace, O Lord, in all the world;
For only in you can we live in safety.
Lord, keep this nation under your care;

And guide us in the way of justice and truth.
Let your way be known upon earth;
Your saving health among all nations.
Let not the needy, O Lord, be forgotten;
Nor the hope of the poor be taken away.
Create in us clean hearts, O God;
And sustain us with your Holy Spirit.

The disciples inquired, "Lord, teach us to pray." We join with his reply.

THE LORD'S PRAYER

Our Father, who art in heaven, hallowed be thy name. Thy Kingdom come, thy will be done, on earth as it is in heaven. Give us this day our daily bread. And forgive us our trespasses, as we forgive those who trespass against us. And lead us not into temptation, but deliver us from evil.

Spend a few moments in silence, meditating on the Lord.

CONCLUDING PRAYER

Most Holy God, you have baptized all who believe in you with the same Spirit, into the same body, of which your Son, Jesus Christ, is the head. Grant us now the unity that you desire, so that we all may be one body, in one spirit. In the blessed name of your Son, our Lord Jesus Christ, and in the fellowship of the Holy Spirit, amen.

Quiet your heart before the Lord, then proceed as you feel ready.

Ascribe to the LORD
   The glory due his name.
Worship the LORD
   In the splendor of his holiness.

Glory to the Father, and to the Son, and to the Holy Spirit. As it was in the beginning, is now, and will be forever: from unending to unending. Amen.

For the mighty works of God, lift your praises.

PSALM 148:1–12
Laudate Dominum

Praise ye the LORD.
   Praise ye the LORD from the heavens:
   praise him in the heights.
Praise ye him, all his angels:
   praise ye him, all his hosts.
Let us praise the LORD.
Praise ye him, sun and moon:
   praise him, all ye stars of light.
Praise him, ye heavens of heavens,
   and ye waters that be above the heavens.
Let them praise the name of the LORD:
   for he commanded, and they were created.
He hath also stablished them for ever and ever:
   he hath made a decree which shall not pass.

Let them praise the LORD.
Praise the LORD from the earth,
    ye dragons, and all deeps:
Fire, and hail; snow, and vapour;
    stormy wind fulfilling his word:
Mountains, and all hills;
    fruitful trees, and all cedars:
Beasts, and all cattle;
    creeping things, and flying fowl:
Kings of the earth, and all people;
    princes, and all judges of the earth:
Both young men, and maidens;
    old men, and children:
Let all voices praise the LORD.

Let us kneel and ask God to cleanse us from all unrighteousness.

PRAYER OF CONFESSION

Most holy and gracious God, we confess to you that we don't always
get it right. We don't always love as you have called us to love. We
don't often enough answer your invitation to serve. We don't continually seek the lost. But Father, you get it right with us every time.
Accept our humble confession, and sanctify us by the power and
beauty of your Word, that we may live in the light of your goodness,
serve with the warmth of your gentleness, and love with the passion
of your grace. Forever and ever, let it be so.

Pause for a moment to reflect on your repentance.

Then join with the psalmist's heart, giving praise and adoration.

PSALM 98
Cantate Domino

O sing unto the LORD a new song;
    for he hath done marvellous things:
    his right hand, and his holy arm,

hath gotten him the victory.
The LORD hath made known his salvation:
>   his righteousness hath he openly shewed in the sight of
>   >   the heathen.
He hath remembered his mercy
>   and his truth toward the house of Israel:
>   all the ends of the earth have seen the salvation of our God.
Make a joyful noise unto the LORD, all the earth:
>   make a loud noise, and rejoice, and sing praise.
Sing unto the LORD with the harp;
>   with the harp, and the voice of a psalm.
With trumpets and sound of cornet
>   make a joyful noise before the LORD, the King.
Let the sea roar, and the fulness thereof;
>   the world, and they that dwell therein.
Let the floods clap their hands:
>   let the hills be joyful together Before the LORD;
>   for he cometh to judge the earth:
>   with righteousness shall he judge the world,
>   and the people with equity.

Open your ears to hear the Word of the Lord.

A READING FROM SACRED SCRIPTURE
Isaiah 45:3–9 (NCV)

I will give you the wealth that is stored away
>   and the hidden riches
so you will know I am the LORD,
>   the God of Israel, who calls you by name.
I do these things for my servants, the people of Jacob,
>   and for my chosen people, the Israelites.
Cyrus, I call you by name,
>   and I give you a title of honor even though you don't know me.
I am the LORD. There is no other God;
>   I am the only God.
I will make you strong,

even though you don't know me,
so that everyone will know
    there is no other God.
From the east to the west they will know
    I alone am the LORD.
I made the light and the darkness.
    I bring peace, and I cause troubles.
    I, the LORD, do all these things.
"Sky above, make victory fall like rain;
    clouds, pour down victory.
Let the earth receive it,
    and let salvation grow,
and let victory grow with it.
    I, the LORD, have created it.
"How terrible it will be for those who argue with the God
    who made them.
    They are like a piece of broken pottery among many pieces.
The clay does not ask the potter,
    'What are you doing?'
The thing that is made doesn't say to its maker,
    'You have no hands.'"

The Word of the Lord.
Thanks be to God.

Pray now for your own needs and for the needs of others.

Allot ample time to freely express your prayers.

INTERCESSION

How wonderful are you, our God;
    How infinite is your wisdom.
You cover us with arms of grace;
    You protect us, your children.
Great are your ways, O Lord;
    Great, your unending love for us.

Forever we will offer you
All of our praise.
For you are full of compassion
And show mercy to your servants.

The disciples inquired, "Lord, teach us to pray." We join with his reply.

THE LORD'S PRAYER

Our Father, who art in heaven, hallowed be thy name. Thy Kingdom come, thy will be done, on earth as it is in heaven. Give us this day our daily bread. And forgive us our trespasses, as we forgive those who trespass against us. And lead us not into temptation, but deliver us from evil.

Spend a few moments in silence, meditating on the Lord.

CONCLUDING PRAYER

Most Holy God, you have baptized all who believe in you with the same Spirit, into the same body, of which your Son, Jesus Christ, is the head. Grant us now the unity that you desire, so that we all may be one body, in one spirit. In the blessed name of your Son, our Lord Jesus Christ, and in the fellowship of the Holy Spirit, amen.

DAY TWENTY-NINE

Quiet your heart before the Lord, then proceed as you feel ready.

Lord, open our lips,
> And our mouths shall proclaim your praise.

Glory to the Father, and to the Son, and to the Holy Spirit. As it was in the beginning, is now, and will be forever: from unending to unending. Amen.

For the mighty works of God, lift your praises.

PSALM 100
Jubilate Deo

Make a joyful noise unto the Lord, all ye lands.
Serve the Lord with gladness:
> come before his presence with singing.

Be joyful in the Lord, all you lands.
Know ye that the Lord he is God:
> it is he that hath made us, and not we ourselves;
> we are his people, and the sheep of his pasture.

Be joyful in the Lord, all you lands.
Enter into his gates with thanksgiving,
> and into his courts with praise:
> be thankful unto him, and bless his name.

Be joyful in the Lord, all you lands.
For the Lord is good; his mercy is everlasting;
> and his truth endureth to all generations.

His love and mercy endure forever.

Let us kneel and ask God to cleanse us from all unrighteousness.

PRAYER OF CONFESSION

Most holy and gracious God, we confess to you that we don't always get it right. We don't always love as you have called us to love. We don't often enough answer your invitation to serve. We don't continually seek the lost. But Father, you get it right with us every time. Accept our humble confession, and sanctify us by the power and beauty of your Word, that we may live in the light of your goodness, serve with the warmth of your gentleness, and love with the passion of your grace. Forever and ever, let it be so.

Pause for a moment to reflect on your repentance.

Then join with the psalmist's heart, giving praise and adoration.

PSALM 99
Dominus Regnavit

The LORD reigneth;
    let the people tremble:
    he sitteth between the cherubims;
    let the earth be moved.
The LORD is great in Zion;
    and he is high above all the people.
Let them praise thy great and terrible name;
    for it is holy.
The king's strength also loveth judgment;
    thou dost establish equity,
    thou executest judgment and righteousness in Jacob.
Exalt ye the LORD our God,
    and worship at his footstool;
    for he is holy.
Moses and Aaron among his priests,
    and Samuel among them that call upon his name;
    they called upon the LORD,
    and he answered them.

He spake unto them in the cloudy pillar:
> they kept his testimonies, and the ordinance that he gave
> > them.

Thou answeredst them, O LORD our God:
> thou wast a God that forgavest them,
> though thou tookest vengeance of their inventions.

Exalt the LORD our God,
> and worship at his holy hill;
> for the LORD our God is holy.

Open your ears to hear the Word of the Lord.

A READING FROM SACRED SCRIPTURE
Ephesians 5:1–10 (The Message)

Watch what God does, and then you do it, like children who learn proper behavior from their parents. Mostly what God does is love you. Keep company with him and learn a life of love. Observe how Christ loved us. His love was not cautious but extravagant. He didn't love in order to get something from us but to give everything of himself to us. Love like that.

Don't allow love to turn into lust, setting off a downhill slide into sexual promiscuity, filthy practices, or bullying greed. Though some tongues just love the taste of gossip, those who follow Jesus have better uses for language than that. Don't talk dirty or silly. That kind of talk doesn't fit our style. Thanksgiving is our dialect.

You can be sure that using people or religion or things just for what you can get out of them—the usual variations on idolatry—will get you nowhere, and certainly nowhere near the kingdom of Christ, the kingdom of God.

Don't let yourselves get taken in by religious smooth talk. God gets furious with people who are full of religious sales talk but want nothing to do with him. Don't even hang around people like that.

You groped your way through that murk once, but no longer. You're out in the open now. The bright light of Christ makes your way plain. So no more stumbling around. Get on with it! The good, the right, the true—these are the actions appropriate for daylight hours. Figure out what will please Christ, and then do it.

The Word of the Lord.
Thanks be to God.

Pray now for your own needs and for the needs of others.

Allot ample time to freely express your prayers.

INTERCESSION

Save your people, Lord, and bless your inheritance;
Govern and uphold them, now and always.
Day by day we bless you;
We praise your name forever.
Lord, keep us from all sin today;
Have mercy on us, Lord, have mercy.
Lord, show us your love and mercy;
For we put our trust in you.
In you, Lord, is our hope;
And we shall never hope in vain.

The disciples inquired, "Lord, teach us to pray." We join with his reply.

THE LORD'S PRAYER

Our Father, who art in heaven, hallowed be thy name. Thy Kingdom come, thy will be done, on earth as it is in heaven. Give us this day our daily bread. And forgive us our trespasses, as we forgive those who trespass against us. And lead us not into temptation, but deliver us from evil.

Spend a few moments in silence, meditating on the Lord.

CONCLUDING PRAYER

O God, our Father, there is no one like you in all the world, neither in the heavens nor on the earth. You have kept your covenant with us, your servants, who walk daily in your ways. Teach us how to live, how to live humbly before you, committed to following the way of your will. In the blessed name of your Son, our Lord Jesus Christ, and in the fellowship of the Holy Spirit, amen.

DAY THIRTY

3/13

Quiet your heart before the Lord, then proceed as you feel ready.

May the words of our mouths
    And the meditations of our hearts
Be pleasing in your sight,
    O LORD, our Rock and our Redeemer.

Glory to the Father, and to the Son, and to the Holy Spirit. As it was in the beginning, is now, and will be forever: from unending to unending. Amen.

For the mighty works of God, lift your praises.

PSALM 147:1–9
Laudate Dominnum

Praise ye the LORD:
    for it is good to sing praises unto our God;

for it is pleasant; and praise is comely.
It is good to praise the Lord.
The Lord doth build up Jerusalem:
    he gathereth together the outcasts of Israel.
He healeth the broken in heart,
    and bindeth up their wounds.
The Lord is worthy of praise.
He telleth the number of the stars;
    he calleth them all by their names.
Great is our Lord, and of great power:
    his understanding is infinite.
The Lord lifteth up the meek:
    he casteth the wicked down to the ground.
Our God is great and mighty.
Sing unto the Lord with thanksgiving;
    sing praise upon the harp unto our God:
Who covereth the heaven with clouds,
    who prepareth rain for the earth,
    who maketh grass to grow upon the mountains.
He giveth to the beast his food,
    and to the young ravens which cry.
Sing to the Lord who provides.

Let us kneel and ask God to cleanse us from all unrighteousness.

PRAYER OF CONFESSION

Most holy and gracious God, we confess to you that we don't always get it right. We don't always love as you have called us to love. We don't often enough answer your invitation to serve. We don't continually seek the lost. But Father, you get it right with us every time. Accept our humble confession, and sanctify us by the power and beauty of your Word, that we may live in the light of your goodness, serve with the warmth of your gentleness, and love with the passion of your grace. Forever and ever, let it be so.

Pause for a moment to reflect on your repentance.

Then join with the psalmist's heart, giving praise and adoration.

PSALM 101:1–6
Misericordiam et Judicium

I will sing of mercy and judgment:
    unto thee, O LORD, will I sing.
I will behave myself wisely in a perfect way.
    O when wilt thou come unto me?
    I will walk within my house
    with a perfect heart.
I will set no wicked thing before mine eyes:
    I hate the work of them that turn aside;
    it shall not cleave to me.
A froward heart shall depart from me:
    I will not know a wicked person.
Whoso privily slandereth his neighbour,
    him will I cut off:
    him that hath an high look and a proud heart
    will not I suffer.
Mine eyes shall be upon the faithful of the land,
    that they may dwell with me:
    he that walketh in a perfect way,
    he shall serve me.

Open your ears to hear the Word of the Lord.

A READING FROM SACRED SCRIPTURE
Isaiah 49:6–13 (NCV)

Now he told me,
"You are an important servant to me
    to bring back the tribes of Jacob,
    to bring back the people of Israel who are left alive.
But, more importantly, I will make you a light for all nations
    to show people all over the world the way to be saved."
The LORD who saves you

is the Holy One of Israel.
He speaks to the one who is hated by the people,
    to the servant of rulers.
This is what he says: "Kings will see you and stand to honor you;
    great leaders will bow down before you,
because the LORD can be trusted.
    He is the Holy One of Israel, who has chosen you."
This is what the LORD says:
"At the right time I will hear your prayers.
    On the day of salvation I will help you.
I will protect you,
    and you will be the sign of my agreement with the people.
You will bring back the people to the land
    and give the land that is now ruined back to its owners.
You will tell the prisoners, 'Come out of your prison.'
    You will tell those in darkness, 'Come into the light.'
The people will eat beside the roads,
    and they will find food even on bare hills.
They will not be hungry or thirsty.
    Neither the hot sun nor the desert wind will hurt them.
The God who comforts them will lead them
    and guide them by springs of water.
I will make my mountains into roads,
    and the roads will be raised up.
Look, people are coming to me from far away,
    from the north and from the west,
    from Aswan in southern Egypt."
Heavens and earth, be happy.
    Mountains, shout with joy,
because the LORD comforts his people
    and will have pity on those who suffer.

The Word of the Lord.
    Thanks be to God.

Pray now for your own needs and for the needs of others.

Allot ample time to freely express your prayers.

INTERCESSION

We will exalt your name, O Lord,
> *For you have heard our cries,*
And you have healed us.
> *The Lord has lifted us up from the depths.*
We will sing praises to you our Lord,
> *For your anger is fleeting,*
But your favor lasts forever.
> *The Lord has lifted us up from the depths.*
Our hearts cannot stay silent,
Forever we will give you thanks.
> *The Lord has lifted us up from the depths.*

The disciples inquired, "Lord, teach us to pray." We join with his reply.

THE LORD'S PRAYER

Our Father, who art in heaven, hallowed be thy name. Thy Kingdom come, thy will be done, on earth as it is in heaven. Give us this day our daily bread. And forgive us our trespasses, as we forgive those who trespass against us. And lead us not into temptation, but deliver us from evil.

Spend a few moments in silence, meditating on the Lord.

CONCLUDING PRAYER

O God, our Father, there is no one like you in all the world, neither in the heavens nor on the earth. You have kept your covenant with us, your servants, who walk daily in your ways. Teach us how to live, how to live humbly before you, committed to following the way of your will. In the blessed name of your Son, our Lord Jesus Christ, and in the fellowship of the Holy Spirit, amen.

Quiet your heart before the Lord, then proceed as you feel ready.

Teach us your way, O LORD,
    And we will walk in your truth.
Give us undivided hearts,
    That we may fear your name.
Glory to the Father, and to the Son, and to the Holy Spirit. As it was in the beginning, is now, and will be forever: from unending to unending. Amen.

For the mighty works of God, lift your praises.

PSALM 149:1–4
Cantate Domino

Praise ye the LORD.
    Sing unto the LORD a new song,
    and his praise in the congregation of saints.
Sing to the LORD a new song.
Let Israel rejoice in him that made him:
    let the children of Zion be joyful in their King.
Let them praise his name in the dance:
    let them sing praises unto him with the timbrel and harp.
Make music for the LORD our God.
For the LORD taketh pleasure in his people:
    he will beautify the meek with salvation.
For the LORD saves us.

Let us kneel and ask God to cleanse us from all unrighteousness.

PRAYER OF CONFESSION

Most holy and gracious God, we confess to you that we don't always get it right. We don't always love as you have called us to love. We don't often enough answer your invitation to serve. We don't continually seek the lost. But Father, you get it right with us every time. Accept our humble confession, and sanctify us by the power and beauty of your Word, that we may live in the light of your goodness, serve with the warmth of your gentleness, and love with the passion of your grace. Forever and ever, let it be so.

Pause for a moment to reflect on your repentance.

Then join with the psalmist's heart, giving praise and adoration.

PSALM 102:1–13
Domine, Exaudi

Hear my prayer, O LORD,
    and let my cry come unto thee.
Hide not thy face from me
    in the day when I am in trouble;
    incline thine ear unto me:
    in the day when I call answer me speedily.
For my days are consumed like smoke,
    and my bones are burned as an hearth.
My heart is smitten, and withered like grass;
    so that I forget to eat my bread.
By reason of the voice of my groaning
    my bones cleave to my skin.
I am like a pelican of the wilderness:
    I am like an owl of the desert.
I watch, and am
    as a sparrow alone upon the house top.
Mine enemies reproach me all the day;
    and they that are mad against me are sworn against me.
For I have eaten ashes like bread,

and mingled my drink with weeping.
Because of thine indignation and thy wrath:
  for thou hast lifted me up, and cast me down.
My days are like a shadow that declineth;
  and I am withered like grass.
But thou, O Lord, shall endure for ever;
  and thy remembrance unto all generations.
Thou shalt arise, and have mercy upon Zion:
  for the time to favour her, yea,
  the set time, is come.

Open your ears to hear the Word of the Lord.

A READING FROM SACRED SCRIPTURE
Isaiah 51:12–16 (NCV)

The Lord says, "I am the one who comforts you.
  So why should you be afraid of people, who die?
  Why should you fear people who die like the grass?
Have you forgotten the Lord who made you,
  who stretched out the skies
  and made the earth?
Why are you always afraid
  of those angry people who trouble you
  and who want to destroy?
But where are those angry people now?
  People in prison will soon be set free;
they will not die in prison,
  and they will have enough food.
I am the Lord your God,
  who stirs the sea and makes the waves roar.
  My name is the Lord All-Powerful.
I will give you the words I want you to say.
  I will cover you with my hands and protect you.
I made the heavens and the earth,
  and I say to Jerusalem, 'You are my people.'"

The Word of the Lord.
Thanks be to God.

Pray now for your own needs and for the needs of others.

Allot ample time to freely express your prayers.

INTERCESSION

The earth is yours and everything in it,
King of Glory, hear our prayers.
You founded it upon the sea, upon the waters;
King of Glory, hear our prayers.
You clean our hands from the dirt of our sin;
King of Glory, hear our prayers.
You lead us up the mountain, your holy hill;
King of Glory, hear our prayers.
Who is this King of Glory?
The Lord Almighty—he will hear our prayers.

The disciples inquired, "Lord, teach us to pray." We join with his reply.

THE LORD'S PRAYER

Our Father, who art in heaven, hallowed be thy name. Thy Kingdom come, thy will be done, on earth as it is in heaven. Give us this day our daily bread. And forgive us our trespasses, as we forgive those who trespass against us. And lead us not into temptation, but deliver us from evil.

Spend a few moments in silence, meditating on the Lord.

CONCLUDING PRAYER

O God, our Father, there is no one like you in all the world, neither in the heavens nor on the earth. You have kept your covenant with us, your servants, who walk daily in your ways. Teach us how to live, how to live humbly before you, committed to following the way of your will. In the blessed name of your Son, our Lord Jesus Christ, and in the fellowship of the Holy Spirit, amen.

Quiet your heart before the Lord, then proceed as you feel ready.

Give thanks to the LORD,
    And call upon his name.
Make known among the nations
    The great works he has done.
Glory to the Father, and to the Son, and to the Holy Spirit. As it was in the beginning, is now, and will be forever: from unending to unending. Amen.

For the mighty works of God, lift your praises.

PSALM 95:1–7
Venite Exultemus

O come, let us sing unto the LORD:
    let us make a joyful noise to the rock of our salvation.
Let us come before his presence with thanksgiving,
    and make a joyful noise unto him with psalms.
Let us shout to the Rock.
For the LORD is a great God,
    and a great King above all gods.
In his hand are the deep places of the earth:

the strength of the hills is his also.
The sea is his, and he made it:
> and his hands formed the dry land.

Let us worship our Lord, our Creator.

O come, let us worship and bow down:
> let us kneel before the LORD our maker.

For he is our God;
> and we are the people of his pasture,
> and the sheep of his hand.

For he is the Great Shepherd.

Let us kneel and ask God to cleanse us from all unrighteousness.

PRAYER OF CONFESSION

Most holy and gracious God, we confess to you that we don't always get it right. We don't always love as you have called us to love. We don't often enough answer your invitation to serve. We don't continually seek the lost. But Father, you get it right with us every time. Accept our humble confession, and sanctify us by the power and beauty of your Word, that we may live in the light of your goodness, serve with the warmth of your gentleness, and love with the passion of your grace. Forever and ever, let it be so.

Pause for a moment to reflect on your repentance.

Then join with the psalmist's heart, giving praise and adoration.

PSALM 103:1–12

Benedic, Anima Mea

Bless the LORD, O my soul:
> and all that is within me, bless his holy name.

Bless the LORD, O my soul,
> and forget not all his benefits:

Who forgiveth all thine iniquities;
> who healeth all thy diseases;

Who redeemeth thy life from destruction;

who crowneth thee with lovingkindness and tender mercies;
Who satisfieth thy mouth with good things;
    so that thy youth is renewed like the eagle's.
The LORD executeth righteousness
    and judgment for all that are oppressed.
He made known his ways unto Moses,
    his acts unto the children of Israel.
The LORD is merciful and gracious,
    slow to anger, and plenteous in mercy.
He will not always chide:
    neither will he keep his anger for ever.
He hath not dealt with us after our sins;
    nor rewarded us according to our iniquities.
For as the heaven is high above the earth,
    so great is his mercy toward them that fear him.
As far as the east is from the west,
    so far hath he removed our transgressions from us.

Open your ears to hear the Word of the Lord.

A READING FROM SACRED SCRIPTURE
Romans 12:1–8 (NIV)

Therefore, I urge you, brothers, in view of God's mercy, to offer your bodies as living sacrifices, holy and pleasing to God—this is your spiritual act of worship. Do not conform any longer to the pattern of this world, but be transformed by the renewing of your mind. Then you will be able to test and approve what God's will is—his good, pleasing and perfect will.

For by the grace given me I say to every one of you: Do not think of yourself more highly than you ought, but rather think of yourself with sober judgment, in accordance with the measure of faith God has given you. Just as each of us has one body with many members, and these members do not all have the same function, so in Christ we who are many form one body, and each member belongs to all the others. We have different gifts, according to the grace given us. If a man's gift is prophesying, let him use it in proportion to his faith. If it is serving, let him serve; if it is teaching, let him teach; if it is encouraging, let him encourage; if it is contributing to the needs of others, let him give generously; if it is leadership, let him govern diligently; if it is showing mercy, let him do it cheerfully.

The Word of the Lord.
Thanks be to God.

Pray now for your own needs and for the needs of others.

Allot ample time to freely express your prayers.

INTERCESSION

Blessed are the poor in spirit,
For theirs is the kingdom of heaven.
Blessed are those who mourn,
For they will be comforted.
Blessed are the meek,
For they will inherit the earth.
Blessed are those who hunger for righteousness,
For they will be filled.
Blessed are the merciful,
For they will be shown mercy.
Blessed are the pure in heart,
For they will see God.
Blessed are the peacemakers,
For they will be called sons of God.

The disciples inquired, "Lord, teach us to pray." We join with his reply.

THE LORD'S PRAYER

Our Father, who art in heaven, hallowed be thy name. Thy Kingdom come, thy will be done, on earth as it is in heaven. Give us this day our daily bread. And forgive us our trespasses, as we forgive those who trespass against us. And lead us not into temptation, but deliver us from evil.

Spend a few moments in silence, meditating on the Lord.

CONCLUDING PRAYER

O God, our Father, there is no one like you in all the world, neither in the heavens nor on the earth. You have kept your covenant with us, your servants, who walk daily in your ways. Teach us how to live, how to live humbly before you, committed to following the way of your will. In the blessed name of your Son, our Lord Jesus Christ, and in the fellowship of the Holy Spirit, amen.

DAY THIRTY-THREE

Make the sign of the cross over your lips.

From the rising of the sun,
    The name of the LORD is to be praised.
To the place where it sets,
    The name of the LORD is to be praised.

Glory to the Father, and to the Son, and to the Holy Spirit. As it was in the beginning, is now, and will be forever: from unending to unending. Amen.

For the mighty works of God, lift your praises.

PSALM 146:1–8

Lauda, Anima Mea

Praise ye the LORD.
    Praise the LORD, O my soul.
While I live will I praise the LORD:
    I will sing praises unto my God while I have any being.
Praise the LORD, O my soul.
Put not your trust in princes,
    nor in the son of man, in whom there is no help.
His breath goeth forth, he returneth to his earth;
    in that very day his thoughts perish.
Praise the LORD, O my soul.
Happy is he that hath the God of Jacob for his help,
    whose hope is in the LORD his God:
Which made heaven, and earth,
    the sea, and all that therein is:
    which keepeth truth for ever:
Praise the LORD, O my soul.
Which executeth judgment for the oppressed:
    which giveth food to the hungry.
The LORD looseth the prisoners:
The LORD openeth the eyes of the blind:
    the LORD raiseth them that are bowed down:
    the LORD loveth the righteous:
Praise the LORD, O my soul.

Let us kneel and ask God to cleanse us from all unrighteousness.

PRAYER OF CONFESSION

Most holy and gracious God, we confess to you that we don't always get it right. We don't always love as you have called us to love. We don't often enough answer your invitation to serve. We don't continually seek the lost. But Father, you get it right with us every time. Accept our humble confession, and sanctify us by the power and beauty of your Word, that we may live in the light of your goodness, serve with the warmth of your gentleness, and love with the passion of your grace. Forever and ever, let it be so.

Pause for a moment to reflect on your repentance.

Then join with the psalmist's heart, giving praise and adoration.

PSALM 104:1–9

Benedic, Anima Mea

Bless the LORD, O my soul.
> O LORD my God, thou art very great;
> thou art clothed with honour and majesty.

Who coverest thyself with light as with a garment:
> who stretchest out the heavens like a curtain:

Who layeth the beams of his chambers in the waters:
> who maketh the clouds his chariot:
> who walketh upon the wings of the wind:

Who maketh his angels spirits;
> his ministers a flaming fire:

Who laid the foundations of the earth,
> that it should not be removed for ever.

Thou coveredst it with the deep as with a garment:
> the waters stood above the mountains.

At thy rebuke they fled;
> at the voice of thy thunder they hasted away.

They go up by the mountains;
> they go down by the valleys
> unto the place which thou hast founded for them.

Thou hast set a bound that they may not pass over;
> that they turn not again to cover the earth.

Open your ears to hear the Word of the Lord.

A READING FROM SACRED SCRIPTURE

Isaiah 52:4–10 (NCV)

This is what the Lord GOD says:
"First my people went down to Egypt to live.
    Later Assyria made them slaves.
"Now see what has happened," says the LORD.
    "Another nation has taken away my people for nothing.
This nation who rules them makes fun of me," says the LORD.
    "All day long they speak against me.
This has happened so my people will know who I am,
    and so, on that future day, they will know
that I am the one speaking to them.
    It will really be me."
How beautiful is the person
    who comes over the mountains to bring good news,
who announces peace
    and brings good news,
    who announces salvation
and says to Jerusalem,
    "Your God is King."
Listen! Your guards are shouting.
    They are all shouting for joy!
They all will see with their own eyes
    when the LORD returns to Jerusalem.
Jerusalem, your buildings are destroyed now,
    but shout and rejoice together,
because the LORD has comforted his people.
    He has saved Jerusalem.
The LORD will show his holy power
    to all the nations.
Then everyone on earth
    will see the salvation of our God.

The Word of the Lord.
Thanks be to God.

Pray now for your own needs and for the needs of others.

Allot ample time to freely express your prayers.

INTERCESSION

Cleanse me with hyssop, and I will be clean;
    Wash me, and I will be whiter than snow.
Hide your face from my sins
    And blot out all my iniquity.
Create in me a pure heart, O God,
    And renew a steadfast spirit within me.
Do not cast me from your presence
    Or take your Holy Spirit from me.
Restore to me the joy of your salvation
    And grant me a willing spirit, to sustain me.

The disciples inquired, "Lord, teach us to pray." We join with his reply.

THE LORD'S PRAYER

Our Father, who art in heaven, hallowed be thy name. Thy Kingdom come, thy will be done, on earth as it is in heaven. Give us this day our daily bread. And forgive us our trespasses, as we forgive those who trespass against us. And lead us not into temptation, but deliver us from evil.

Spend a few moments in silence, meditating on the Lord.

CONCLUDING PRAYER

O God, our Father, there is no one like you in all the world, neither in the heavens nor on the earth. You have kept your covenant with us, your servants, who walk daily in your ways. Teach us how to live, how to live humbly before you, committed to following the way of your will. In the blessed name of your Son, our Lord Jesus Christ, and in the fellowship of the Holy Spirit, amen.

DAY THIRTY-FOUR

Quiet your heart before the Lord, then proceed as you feel ready.

Love the LORD,
> All you his saints.
Love the LORD your God,
> All you his faithful.

Glory to the Father, and to the Son, and to the Holy Spirit. As it was in the beginning, is now, and will be forever: from unending to unending. Amen.

For the mighty works of God, lift your praises.

PSALM 67
Deus Misereatur

God be merciful unto us, and bless us;
> and cause his face to shine upon us;
> Selah.
That thy way may be known upon earth,
> thy saving health among all nations.
O God, shine upon us.
Let the people praise thee, O God;
> let all the people praise thee.
O let the nations be glad and sing for joy:
> for thou shalt judge the people righteously,
> and govern the nations upon earth.
> Selah.
Let the people praise thee, O God;

let all the people praise thee.
O God, may we, your people, praise you.
Then shall the earth yield her increase;
    and God, even our own God, shall bless us.
God shall bless us;
    and all the ends of the earth shall fear him.
O God, may we, your people, praise you.

Let us kneel and ask God to cleanse us from all unrighteousness.

PRAYER OF CONFESSION

Most holy and gracious God, we confess to you that we don't always get it right. We don't always love as you have called us to love. We don't often enough answer your invitation to serve. We don't continually seek the lost. But Father, you get it right with us every time. Accept our humble confession, and sanctify us by the power and beauty of your Word, that we may live in the light of your goodness, serve with the warmth of your gentleness, and love with the passion of your grace. Forever and ever, let it be so.

Pause for a moment to reflect on your repentance.

Then join with the psalmist's heart, giving praise and adoration.

PSALM 105:1–11
Confitemini Domino

O give thanks unto the LORD; call upon his name:
    make known his deeds among the people.
Sing unto him, sing psalms unto him:
    talk ye of all his wondrous works.
Glory ye in his holy name:
    let the heart of them rejoice that seek the LORD.
Seek the LORD, and his strength:
    seek his face evermore.
Remember his marvellous works that he hath done;
    his wonders, and the judgments of his mouth;

O ye seed of Abraham his servant,
ye children of Jacob his chosen.
He is the LORD our God:
his judgments are in all the earth.
He hath remembered his covenant for ever,
the word which he commanded to a thousand generations.
Which covenant he made with Abraham,
and his oath unto Isaac;
And confirmed the same unto Jacob for a law,
and to Israel for an everlasting covenant:
Saying, Unto thee will I give the land of Canaan,
the lot of your inheritance.

Open your ears to hear the Word of the Lord.

A READING FROM SACRED SCRIPTURE
Romans 12:9–21 (NIV)

Love must be sincere. Hate what is evil; cling to what is good. Be devoted to one another in brotherly love. Honor one another above yourselves. Never be lacking in zeal, but keep your spiritual fervor, serving the Lord. Be joyful in hope, patient in affliction, faithful in prayer. Share with God's people who are in need. Practice hospitality.

Bless those who persecute you; bless and do not curse. Rejoice with those who rejoice; mourn with those who mourn. Live in harmony with one another. Do not be proud, but be willing to associate with people of low position. Do not be conceited.

Do not repay anyone evil for evil. Be careful to do what is right in the eyes of everybody. If it is possible, as far as it depends on you, live at peace with everyone. Do not take revenge, my friends, but leave room for God's wrath, for it is written: "It is mine to avenge; I will repay," says the Lord. On the contrary:
"If your enemy is hungry, feed him;
if he is thirsty, give him something to drink.
In doing this, you will heap burning coals on his head."
Do not be overcome by evil, but overcome evil with good.

The Word of the Lord.
Thanks be to God.

Pray now for your own needs and for the needs of others.

Allot ample time to freely express your prayers.

INTERCESSION

Show us your mercy, O Lord;
And grant us your salvation.
Clothe your ministers with righteousness;
Let your people sing with joy.
Give peace, O Lord, in all the world;
For only in you can we live in safety.
Lord, keep this nation under your care;
And guide us in the way of justice and truth.
Let your way be known upon earth;
Your saving health among all nations.
Let not the needy, O Lord, be forgotten;
Nor the hope of the poor be taken away.
Create in us clean hearts, O God;
And sustain us with your Holy Spirit.

The disciples inquired, "Lord, teach us to pray." We join with his reply.

THE LORD'S PRAYER

Our Father, who art in heaven, hallowed be thy name. Thy Kingdom come, thy will be done, on earth as it is in heaven. Give us this day our daily bread. And forgive us our trespasses, as we forgive those who trespass against us. And lead us not into temptation, but deliver us from evil.

Spend a few moments in silence, meditating on the Lord.

CONCLUDING PRAYER

O God, our Father, there is no one like you in all the world, neither in the heavens nor on the earth. You have kept your covenant with us, your servants, who walk daily in your ways. Teach us how to live, how to live humbly before you, committed to following the way of your will. In the blessed name of your Son, our Lord Jesus Christ, and in the fellowship of the Holy Spirit, amen.

Quiet your heart before the Lord, then proceed as you feel ready.

Ascribe to the LORD
    The glory due his name.
Worship the LORD
    In the splendor of his holiness.
Glory to the Father, and to the Son, and to the Holy Spirit. As it was in the beginning, is now, and will be forever: from unending to unending. Amen.

For the mighty works of God, lift your praises.

PSALM 148:1–12
Laudate Dominum

Praise ye the LORD.
    Praise ye the LORD from the heavens:
    praise him in the heights.

Praise ye him, all his angels:
  praise ye him, all his hosts.
Let us praise the LORD.
Praise ye him, sun and moon:
  praise him, all ye stars of light.
Praise him, ye heavens of heavens,
  and ye waters that be above the heavens.
Let them praise the name of the LORD:
  for he commanded, and they were created.
He hath also stablished them for ever and ever:
  he hath made a decree which shall not pass.
Let them praise the LORD.
Praise the LORD from the earth,
  ye dragons, and all deeps:
Fire, and hail; snow, and vapour;
  stormy wind fulfilling his word:
Mountains, and all hills;
  fruitful trees, and all cedars:
Beasts, and all cattle;
  creeping things, and flying fowl:
Kings of the earth, and all people;
  princes, and all judges of the earth:
Both young men, and maidens;
  old men, and children:
Let all voices praise the LORD.

Let us kneel and ask God to cleanse us from all unrighteousness.

PRAYER OF CONFESSION

Most holy and gracious God, we confess to you that we don't
always get it right. We don't always love as you have called us to
love. We don't often enough answer your invitation to serve. We
don't continually seek the lost. But Father, you get it right with us
every time. Accept our humble confession, and sanctify us by the
power and beauty of your Word, that we may live in the light of

your goodness, serve with the warmth of your gentleness, and love
with the passion of your grace. Forever and ever, let it be so.

Pause for a moment to reflect on your repentance.

Then join with the psalmist's heart, giving praise and adoration.

PSALM 106:1–8
Confitemini Domino

Praise ye the LORD.
> O give thanks unto the LORD; for he is good:
> for his mercy endureth for ever.
Who can utter the mighty acts of the LORD?
> who can shew forth all his praise?
Blessed are they that keep judgment,
> and he that doeth righteousness at all times.
Remember me, O LORD, with the favour that thou bearest
> unto thy people:
> O visit me with thy salvation;
That I may see the good of thy chosen,
> that I may rejoice in the gladness of thy nation,
> that I may glory with thine inheritance.
We have sinned with our fathers,
> we have committed iniquity, we have done wickedly.
Our fathers understood not thy wonders in Egypt;
> they remembered not the multitude of thy mercies;
> but provoked him at the sea, even at the Red sea.
Nevertheless he saved them for his name's sake,
> that he might make his mighty power to be known.

Open your ears to hear the Word of the Lord.

A READING FROM SACRED SCRIPTURE
Isaiah 53:1–12 (NCV)

Who would have believed what we heard?
Who saw the LORD's power in this?

He grew up like a small plant before the LORD,
    like a root growing in a dry land.
He had no special beauty or form to make us notice him;
    there was nothing in his appearance to make us desire him.
He was hated and rejected by people.
    He had much pain and suffering.
People would not even look at him.
    He was hated, and we didn't even notice him.
But he took our suffering on him
    and felt our pain for us.
We saw his suffering
    and thought God was punishing him.
But he was wounded for the wrong we did;
    he was crushed for the evil we did.
The punishment, which made us well, was given to him,
    and we are healed because of his wounds.
We all have wandered away like sheep;
    each of us has gone his own way.
But the LORD has put on him the punishment
    for all the evil we have done.
He was beaten down and punished,
    but he didn't say a word.
He was like a lamb being led to be killed.
    He was quiet, as a sheep is quiet while its wool is being cut;
    he never opened his mouth.
Men took him away roughly and unfairly.
    He died without children to continue his family.
He was put to death;
    he was punished for the sins of my people.
He was buried with wicked men,
    and he died with the rich.
He had done nothing wrong,
    and he had never lied.
But it was the LORD who decided
    to crush him and make him suffer.
    The LORD made his life a penalty offering,

but he will still see his descendants and live a long life.
    He will complete the things the LORD wants him to do.
"After his soul suffers many things,
    he will see life and be satisfied.
My good servant will make many people right with God;
    he will carry away their sins.
For this reason I will make him a great man among people,
    and he will share in all things with those who are strong.
He willingly gave his life
    and was treated like a criminal.
But he carried away the sins of many people
    and asked forgiveness for those who sinned."

The Word of the Lord.
Thanks be to God.

Pray now for your own needs and for the needs of others.

Allot ample time to freely express your prayers.

INTERCESSION

How wonderful are you, our God;
    How infinite is your wisdom.
You cover us with arms of grace;
    You protect us, your children.
Great are your ways, O Lord;
    Great, your unending love for us.
Forever we will offer you
    All of our praise.
For you are full of compassion
    And show mercy to your servants.

The disciples inquired, "Lord, teach us to pray." We join with his reply.

THE LORD'S PRAYER

Our Father, who art in heaven, hallowed be thy name. Thy Kingdom come, thy will be done, on earth as it is in heaven. Give us this day our daily bread. And forgive us our trespasses, as we forgive those who trespass against us. And lead us not into temptation, but deliver us from evil.

Spend a few moments in silence, meditating on the Lord.

CONCLUDING PRAYER

O God, our Father, there is no one like you in all the world, neither in the heavens nor on the earth. You have kept your covenant with us, your servants, who walk daily in your ways. Teach us how to live, how to live humbly before you, committed to following the way of your will. In the blessed name of your Son, our Lord Jesus Christ, and in the fellowship of the Holy Spirit, amen.

DAY THIRTY-SIX

Quiet your heart before the Lord, then proceed as you feel ready.

LORD, open our lips,
    And our mouths shall proclaim your praise.

Glory to the Father, and to the Son, and to the Holy Spirit. As it was in the beginning, is now, and will be forever: from unending to unending. Amen.

For the mighty works of God, lift your praises.

PSALM 100

Jubilate Deo

Make a joyful noise unto the LORD, all ye lands.
Serve the LORD with gladness:
    come before his presence with singing.
Be joyful in the LORD, all you lands.
Know ye that the LORD he is God:
    it is he that hath made us, and not we ourselves;
    we are his people, and the sheep of his pasture.
Be joyful in the LORD, all you lands.
Enter into his gates with thanksgiving,
    and into his courts with praise:
    be thankful unto him, and bless his name.
Be joyful in the LORD, all you lands.
For the LORD is good; his mercy is everlasting;
    and his truth endureth to all generations.
His love and mercy endure forever.

Let us kneel and ask God to cleanse us from all unrighteousness.

PRAYER OF CONFESSION

Most holy and gracious God, we confess to you that we don't always get it right. We don't always love as you have called us to love. We don't often enough answer your invitation to serve. We don't continually seek the lost. But Father, you get it right with us every time. Accept our humble confession, and sanctify us by the power and beauty of your Word, that we may live in the light of your goodness, serve with the warmth of your gentleness, and love with the passion of your grace. Forever and ever, let it be so.

Pause for a moment to reflect on your repentance.

Then join with the psalmist's heart, giving praise and adoration.

PSALM 34:1–9

Benedicam Dominum

I will bless the LORD at all times:
    his praise shall continually be in my mouth.
My soul shall make her boast in the LORD:
    the humble shall hear thereof, and be glad.
O magnify the LORD with me,
    and let us exalt his name together.
I sought the LORD, and he heard me,
    and delivered me from all my fears.
They looked unto him, and were lightened:
    and their faces were not ashamed.
This poor man cried, and the LORD heard him,
    and saved him out of all his troubles.
The angel of the LORD encampeth round about them that fear
      him,
    and delivereth them.
O taste and see that the LORD is good:
    blessed is the man that trusteth in him.
O fear the LORD, ye his saints:
    for there is no want to them that fear him.

Open your ears to hear the Word of the Lord.

A READING FROM SACRED SCRIPTURE
Ephesians 6:10–20 (The Message)

And that about wraps it up. God is strong, and he wants you strong. So take everything the Master has set out for you, well-made weapons of the best materials. And put them to use so you will be able to stand up to everything the Devil throws your way. This is no afternoon athletic contest that we'll walk away from and forget about in a couple of hours. This is for keeps, a life-or-death fight to the finish against the Devil and all his angels.

Be prepared. You're up against far more than you can handle on your own. Take all the help you can get, every weapon God has issued, so that when it's all over but the shouting you'll still be on your feet. Truth, righteousness, peace, faith, and salvation are more than words. Learn how to apply them. You'll need them throughout your life. God's Word is an indispensable weapon. In the same way, prayer is essential in this ongoing warfare. Pray hard and long. Pray for your brothers and sisters. Keep your eyes open. Keep each other's spirits up so that no one falls behind or drops out.

And don't forget to pray for me. Pray that I'll know what to say and have the courage to say it at the right time, telling the mystery to one and all, the Message that I, jailbird preacher that I am, am responsible for getting out.

The Word of the Lord.
Thanks be to God.

Pray now for your own needs and for the needs of others.

Allot ample time to freely express your prayers.

INTERCESSION

Save your people, Lord, and bless your inheritance;
Govern and uphold them, now and always.
Day by day we bless you;
We praise your name forever.
Lord, keep us from all sin today;
Have mercy on us, Lord, have mercy.
Lord, show us your love and mercy;
For we put our trust in you.
In you, Lord, is our hope;
And we shall never hope in vain.

The disciples inquired, "Lord, teach us to pray." We join with his reply.

THE LORD'S PRAYER

Our Father, who art in heaven, hallowed be thy name. Thy Kingdom come, thy will be done, on earth as it is in heaven. Give us this day our daily bread. And forgive us our trespasses, as we forgive those who trespass against us. And lead us not into temptation, but deliver us from evil.

Spend a few moments in silence, meditating on the Lord.

CONCLUDING PRAYER

Gracious Father, humbly your Son came into this world, not to condemn but to heal, to bring life overflowing, the fullness of joy. Set our hearts on our Savior; direct our wills to follow him as we humbly obey your righteous commands. In the blessed name of your Son, our Lord Jesus Christ, and in the fellowship of the Holy Spirit, amen.

DAY THIRTY-SEVEN

Quiet your heart before the Lord, then proceed as you feel ready.

May the words of our mouths
    And the meditations of our hearts
Be pleasing in your sight,
    O LORD, our Rock and our Redeemer.

Glory to the Father, and to the Son, and to the Holy Spirit. As it was in the beginning, is now, and will be forever: from unending to unending. Amen.

For the mighty works of God, lift your praises.

PSALM 147:1–9

Laudate Dominum

Praise ye the LORD:
>for it is good to sing praises unto our God;
>for it is pleasant; and praise is comely.

It is good to praise the LORD.

The LORD doth build up Jerusalem:
>he gathereth together the outcasts of Israel.

He healeth the broken in heart,
>and bindeth up their wounds.

The LORD is worthy of praise.

He telleth the number of the stars;
>he calleth them all by their names.

Great is our Lord, and of great power:
>his understanding is infinite.

The LORD lifteth up the meek:
>he casteth the wicked down to the ground.

Our God is great and mighty.

Sing unto the LORD with thanksgiving;
>sing praise upon the harp unto our God:

Who covereth the heaven with clouds,
>who prepareth rain for the earth,
>who maketh grass to grow upon the mountains.

He giveth to the beast his food,
>and to the young ravens which cry.

Sing to the LORD who provides.

Let us kneel and ask God to cleanse us from all unrighteousness.

PRAYER OF CONFESSION

Most holy and gracious God, we confess to you that we don't always get it right. We don't always love as you have called us to love. We don't often enough answer your invitation to serve. We don't continually seek the lost. But Father, you get it right with us every time. Accept our humble confession, and sanctify us by the power and beauty of your Word, that we may live in the light of your goodness, serve with the warmth of your gentleness, and love with the passion of your grace. Forever and ever, let it be so.

Pause for a moment to reflect on your repentance.

Then join with the psalmist's heart, giving praise and adoration.

PSALM 36:5–10
Dixit Injustus

Thy mercy, O LORD, is in the heavens;
    and thy faithfulness reacheth unto the clouds.
Thy righteousness is like the great mountains;
    thy judgments are a great deep:
    O LORD, thou preservest man and beast.
How excellent is thy lovingkindness, O God!
    therefore the children of men
    put their trust under the shadow of thy wings.
They shall be abundantly satisfied with the fatness of thy
       house;
    and thou shalt make them drink of the river of thy pleasures.
For with thee is the fountain of life:
    in thy light shall we see light.
O continue thy lovingkindness unto them that know thee;
    and thy righteousness to the upright in heart.

Open your heart to the Word of the Lord.

A READING FROM SACRED SCRIPTURE
Isaiah 59:1–8 (NCV)

Surely the LORD's power is enough to save you.
    He can hear you when you ask him for help.
It is your evil that has separated
    you from your God.
Your sins cause him to turn away from you,

so he does not hear you.
With your hands you have killed others,
    and with your fingers you have done wrong.
With your lips you have lied,
    and with your tongue you say evil things.
People take each other to court unfairly,
    and no one tells the truth in arguing his case.
They accuse each other falsely and tell lies.
    They cause trouble and create more evil.
They hatch evil like eggs from poisonous snakes.
    , If you eat one of those eggs, you will die,
    and if you break one open, a poisonous snake comes out.
People tell lies as they would spin a spider's web.
    The webs they make cannot be used for clothes;
    you can't cover yourself with those webs.
The things they do are evil,
    and they use their hands to hurt others.
They eagerly run to do evil,
    and they are always ready to kill innocent people.
They think evil thoughts.
    Everywhere they go they cause ruin and destruction.
They don't know how to live in peace,
    and there is no fairness in their lives.
They are dishonest.
    Anyone who lives as they live will never have peace.

The Word of the Lord.
Thanks be to God.

Pray now for your own needs and for the needs of others.

Allot ample time to freely express your prayers.

INTERCESSION

We will exalt your name, O Lord,
    For you have heard our cries,

And you have healed us.
The Lord has lifted us up from the depths.
We will sing praises to you our Lord,
For your anger is fleeting,
But your favor lasts forever.
The Lord has lifted us up from the depths.
Our hearts cannot stay silent,
Forever we will give you thanks.
The Lord has lifted us up from the depths.

The disciples inquired, "Lord, teach us to pray." We join with his reply.

THE LORD'S PRAYER

Our Father, who art in heaven, hallowed be thy name. Thy Kingdom come, thy will be done, on earth as it is in heaven. Give us this day our daily bread. And forgive us our trespasses, as we forgive those who trespass against us. And lead us not into temptation, but deliver us from evil.

Spend a few moments in silence, meditating on the Lord.

CONCLUDING PRAYER

Gracious Father, humbly your Son came into this world, not to condemn but to heal, to bring life overflowing, the fullness of joy. Set our hearts on our Savior; direct our wills to follow him as we humbly obey your righteous commands. In the blessed name of your Son, our Lord Jesus Christ, and in the fellowship of the Holy Spirit, amen.

3/21

Quiet your heart before the Lord, then proceed as you feel ready.

Teach us your way, O LORD,
   And we will walk in your truth
Give us undivided hearts,
   That we may fear your name

Glory to the Father, and to the Son, and to the Holy Spirit. As it was in the beginning, is now, and will be forever: from unending to unending. Amen.

For the mighty works of God, lift your praises.

PSALM 149:1–4
Cantate Domino

Praise ye the LORD.
   Sing unto the LORD a new song,
   and his praise in the congregation of saints.
Sing to the LORD a new song.
Let Israel rejoice in him that made him:
   let the children of Zion be joyful in their King.
Let them praise his name in the dance:
   let them sing praises unto him with the timbrel and harp.
Make music for the LORD our God.
For the LORD taketh pleasure in his people:
   he will beautify the meek with salvation.
For the LORD saves us.

Let us kneel and ask God to cleanse us from all unrighteousness.

PRAYER OF CONFESSION

Most holy and gracious God, we confess to you that we don't always get it right. We don't always love as you have called us to love. We don't often enough answer your invitation to serve. We don't continually seek the lost. But Father, you get it right with us every time. Accept our humble confession, and sanctify us by the power and beauty of your Word, that we may live in the light of your goodness, serve with the warmth of your gentleness, and love with the passion of your grace. Forever and ever, let it be so.

Pause for a moment to reflect on your repentance.

Then join with the psalmist's heart, giving praise and adoration.

PSALM 37:1–8
Noli Aemulari

Fret not thyself because of evildoers,
> neither be thou envious against the workers of iniquity.
For they shall soon be cut down like the grass,
> and wither as the green herb.
Trust in the LORD, and do good;
> so shalt thou dwell in the land, and verily thou shalt be fed.
Delight thyself also in the LORD:
> and he shall give thee the desires of thine heart.
Commit thy way unto the LORD;
> trust also in him; and he shall bring it to pass.
And he shall bring forth thy righteousness as the light,
> and thy judgment as the noonday.
Rest in the LORD, and wait patiently for him:
> fret not thyself because of him who prospereth in his way,
> because of the man who bringeth wicked devices to pass.
Cease from anger, and forsake wrath:
> fret not thyself in any wise to do evil.

Open your ears to hear the Word of the Lord.

A READING FROM SACRED SCRIPTURE
Isaiah 55:1–11 (NCV)

The LORD says, "All you who are thirsty,
    come and drink.
Those of you who do not have money,
    come, buy and eat!
Come buy wine and milk
    without money and without cost.
Why spend your money on something that is not real food?
    Why work for something that doesn't really satisfy you?
Listen closely to me, and you will eat what is good;
    your soul will enjoy the rich food that satisfies.
Come to me and listen;
    listen to me so you may live.
I will make an agreement with you that will last forever.
    I will give you the blessings I promised to David.
I made David a witness of my power for all nations,
    a ruler and commander of many nations.
You will call for nations that you don't yet know.
    And these nations that do not know you will run to you
because of the LORD your God,
    because of the Holy One of Israel who honors you."
So you should look for the LORD before it is too late;
    you should call to him while he is near.
The wicked should stop doing wrong,
    and they should stop their evil thoughts.
They should return to the LORD so he may have mercy on them.
    They should come to our God, because he will freely forgive
        them.
The LORD says, "My thoughts are not like your thoughts.
    Your ways are not like my ways.
Just as the heavens are higher than the earth,
    so are my ways higher than your ways

and my thoughts higher than your thoughts.
Rain and snow fall from the sky
   and don't return without watering the ground.
They cause the plants to sprout and grow,
   making seeds for the farmer
   and bread for the people.
The same thing is true of the words I speak.
   They will not return to me empty.
They make the things happen that I want to happen,
   and they succeed in doing what I send them to do."

The Word of the Lord.
Thanks be to God.

Pray now for your own needs and for the needs of others.

Allot ample time to freely express your prayers.

INTERCESSION

The earth is yours and everything in it,
   King of Glory, hear our prayers.
You founded it upon the sea, upon the waters;
   King of Glory, hear our prayers.
You clean our hands from the dirt of our sin;
   King of Glory, hear our prayers.
You lead us up the mountain, your holy hill;
   King of Glory, hear our prayers.
Who is this King of Glory?
   The Lord Almighty—he will hear our prayers.

The disciples inquired, "Lord, teach us to pray." We join with his reply.

THE LORD'S PRAYER

Our Father, who art in heaven, hallowed be thy name. Thy Kingdom
come, thy will be done, on earth as it is in heaven. Give us this day
our daily bread. And forgive us our trespasses, as we forgive those

who trespass against us. And lead us not into temptation, but deliver us from evil.

Spend a few moments in silence, meditating on the Lord.

CONCLUDING PRAYER

Gracious Father, humbly your Son came into this world, not to condemn but to heal, to bring life overflowing, the fullness of joy. Set our hearts on our Savior; direct our wills to follow him as we humbly obey your righteous commands. In the blessed name of your Son, our Lord Jesus Christ, and in the fellowship of the Holy Spirit, amen.

DAY THIRTY-NINE

Quiet your heart before the Lord, then proceed as you feel ready.

Give thanks to the LORD,
    And call upon his name.
Make known among the nations
    The great works he has done.

Glory to the Father, and to the Son, and to the Holy Spirit. As it was in the beginning, is now, and will be forever: from unending to unending. Amen.

For the mighty works of God, lift your praises.

PSALM 95:1–7

Venite Exultemus

O come, let us sing unto the LORD:
  let us make a joyful noise to the rock of our salvation.
Let us come before his presence with thanksgiving,
  and make a joyful noise unto him with psalms.
Let us shout to the Rock.
For the LORD is a great God,
  and a great King above all gods.
In his hand are the deep places of the earth:
  the strength of the hills is his also.
The sea is his, and he made it:
  and his hands formed the dry land.
Let us worship our Lord, our Creator.
O come, let us worship and bow down:
  let us kneel before the LORD our maker.
For he is our God;
  and we are the people of his pasture,
  and the sheep of his hand.
For he is the Great Shepherd.

Let us kneel and ask God to cleanse us from all unrighteousness.

PRAYER OF CONFESSION

Most holy and gracious God, we confess to you that we don't always get it right. We don't always love as you have called us to love. We don't often enough answer your invitation to serve. We don't continually seek the lost. But Father, you get it right with us every time. Accept our humble confession, and sanctify us by the power and beauty of your Word, that we may live in the light of your goodness, serve with the warmth of your gentleness, and love with the passion of your grace. Forever and ever, let it be so.

Pause for a moment to reflect on your repentance.

Then join with the psalmist's heart, giving praise and adoration.

PSALM 39:1–7
Dixi, Custodiam

I said, I will take heed to my ways,
>   that I sin not with my tongue:
>   I will keep my mouth with a bridle,
>   while the wicked is before me.

I was dumb with silence,
>   I held my peace, even from good;
>   and my sorrow was stirred.

My heart was hot within me,
>   while I was musing the fire burned:
>   then spake I with my tongue,

LORD, make me to know mine end,
>   and the measure of my days, what it is:
>   that I may know how frail I am.

Behold, thou hast made my days as an handbreadth;
>   and mine age is as nothing before thee:
>   verily every man at his best state is altogether vanity.
>   Selah.

Surely every man walketh in a vain shew:
>   surely they are disquieted in vain:
>   he heapeth up riches, and knoweth not who shall gather them.

And now, Lord, what wait I for?
>   my hope is in thee.

Open your ears to hear the Word of the Lord.

A READING FROM SACRED SCRIPTURE
Romans 13:8–14 (NIV)

Let no debt remain outstanding, except the continuing debt to love one another, for he who loves his fellowman has fulfilled the law. The commandments, "Do not commit adultery," "Do not murder," "Do not steal," "Do not covet," and whatever other commandment there may be, are summed up in this one rule: "Love your neighbor as yourself." Love does no harm to its neighbor. Therefore love is the fulfillment of the law.

And do this, understanding the present time. The hour has come for you to wake up from your slumber, because our salvation is nearer now than when we first believed. The night is nearly over; the day is almost here. So let us put aside the deeds of darkness and put on the armor of light. Let us behave decently, as in the daytime, not in orgies and drunkenness, not in sexual immorality and debauchery, not in dissension and jealousy. Rather, clothe yourselves with the Lord Jesus Christ, and do not think about how to gratify the desires of the sinful nature.

The Word of the Lord.
Thanks be to God.

Pray now for your own needs and for the needs of others.

Allot ample time to freely express your prayers.

INTERCESSION

Blessed are the poor in spirit,
For theirs is the kingdom of heaven.
Blessed are those who mourn,
For they will be comforted.
Blessed are the meek,
For they will inherit the earth.
Blessed are those who hunger for righteousness,
For they will be filled.
Blessed are the merciful,
For they will be shown mercy.
Blessed are the pure in heart,
For they will see God.
Blessed are the peacemakers,
For they will be called sons of God.

The disciples inquired, "Lord, teach us to pray." We join with his reply.

THE LORD'S PRAYER

Our Father, who art in heaven, hallowed be thy name. Thy Kingdom come, thy will be done, on earth as it is in heaven. Give us this day our daily bread. And forgive us our trespasses, as we forgive those who trespass against us. And lead us not into temptation, but deliver us from evil.

Spend a few moments in silence, meditating on the Lord.

CONCLUDING PRAYER

Gracious Father, humbly your Son came into this world, not to condemn but to heal, to bring life overflowing, the fullness of joy. Set our hearts on our Savior; direct our wills to follow him as we humbly obey your righteous commands. In the blessed name of your Son, our Lord Jesus Christ, and in the fellowship of the Holy Spirit, amen.

3|23

DAY FORTY

Quiet your heart before the Lord, then proceed as you feel ready.

From the rising of the sun,
     The name of the LORD is to be praised.
To the place where it sets,
     The name of the LORD is to be praised.

Glory to the Father, and to the Son, and to the Holy Spirit. As it was in the beginning, is now, and will be forever: from unending to unending. Amen.

For the mighty works of God, lift your praises.

PSALM 146:1–8

Lauda, Anima Mea

Praise ye the LORD.
Praise the LORD, O my soul.
While I live will I praise the LORD:
I will sing praises unto my God while I have any being.
Praise the LORD, O my soul.
Put not your trust in princes,
nor in the son of man, in whom there is no help.
His breath goeth forth, he returneth to his earth;
in that very day his thoughts perish.
Praise the LORD, O my soul.
Happy is he that hath the God of Jacob for his help,
whose hope is in the LORD his God:
Which made heaven, and earth,
the sea, and all that therein is:
which keepeth truth for ever:
Praise the LORD, O my soul.
Which executeth judgment for the oppressed:
which giveth food to the hungry.
The LORD looseth the prisoners:
The LORD openeth the eyes of the blind:
the LORD raiseth them that are bowed down:
the LORD loveth the righteous:
Praise the LORD, O my soul.

Let us kneel and ask God to cleanse us from all unrighteousness.

PRAYER OF CONFESSION

Most holy and gracious God, we confess to you that we don't always get it right. We don't always love as you have called us to love. We don't often enough answer your invitation to serve. We don't continually seek the lost. But Father, you get it right with us every time. Accept our humble confession, and sanctify us by the power and beauty of your Word, that we may live in the light of your goodness, serve with the warmth of your gentleness, and love with the passion of your grace. Forever and ever, let it be so.

Pause for a moment to reflect on your repentance.

Then join with the psalmist's heart, giving praise and adoration.

PSALM 40

Expectans, Expectavi

I waited patiently for the LORD;
    and he inclined unto me, and heard my cry.
He brought me up also out of an horrible pit,
    out of the miry clay,
    and set my feet upon a rock,
    and established my goings.
And he hath put a new song in my mouth,
    even praise unto our God:
    many shall see it, and fear,
    and shall trust in the LORD.
Blessed is that man
    that maketh the LORD his trust,
    and respecteth not the proud,
    nor such as turn aside to lies.
Many, O LORD my God,
    are thy wonderful works which thou hast done,
    and thy thoughts which are to us-ward:
    they cannot be reckoned up in order unto thee:
    if I would declare and speak of them,
    they are more than can be numbered.

Sacrifice and offering thou didst not desire;
    mine ears hast thou opened:
    burnt offering and sin offering
    hast thou not required.
Then said I, Lo, I come:
    in the volume of the book it is written of me,
I delight to do thy will, O my God:
    yea, thy law is within my heart.

Open your ears to hear the Word of the Lord.

A READING FROM SACRED SCRIPTURE
Isaiah 65:17–25 (NCV)

"Look, I will make new heavens and a new earth,
    and people will not remember the past
    or think about those things.
My people will be happy forever
    because of the things I will make.
I will make a Jerusalem that is full of joy,
    and I will make her people a delight.
Then I will rejoice over Jerusalem
    and be delighted with my people.
There will never again be heard in that city
    the sounds of crying and sadness.
There will never be a baby from that city
    who lives only a few days.
And there will never be an older person
    who doesn't have a long life.
A person who lives a hundred years will be called young,
    and a person who dies before he is a hundred will be
        thought of as a sinner.
In that city those who build houses will live there.
    Those who plant vineyards will get to eat their grapes.
No more will one person build a house and someone else live there.
    One person will not plant a garden and someone else eat its
        fruit.

My people will live a long time,
as trees live long.
My chosen people will live there
and enjoy the things they make.
They will never again work for nothing.
They will never again give birth to children who die young.
All my people will be blessed by the LORD;
they and their children will be blessed.
I will provide for their needs before they ask,
and I will help them while they are still asking for help.
Wolves and lambs will eat together in peace.
Lions will eat hay like oxen,
and a snake on the ground will not hurt anyone.
They will not hurt or destroy each other
on all my holy mountain,"
says the LORD.

The Word of the Lord.
Thanks be to God.

Pray now for your own needs and for the needs of others.

Allot ample time to freely express your prayers.

INTERCESSION

Cleanse me with hyssop, and I will be clean;
Wash me, and I will be whiter than snow.
Hide your face from my sins
And blot out all my iniquity.
Create in me a pure heart, O God,
And renew a steadfast spirit within me.
Do not cast me from your presence
Or take your Holy Spirit from me.
Restore to me the joy of your salvation
And grant me a willing spirit, to sustain me.

The disciples inquired, "Lord, teach us to pray." We join with his reply.

THE LORD'S PRAYER

Our Father, who art in heaven, hallowed be thy name. Thy Kingdom come, thy will be done, on earth as it is in heaven. Give us this day our daily bread. And forgive us our trespasses, as we forgive those who trespass against us. And lead us not into temptation, but deliver us from evil.

Spend a few moments in silence, meditating on the Lord.

CONCLUDING PRAYER

Gracious Father, humbly your Son came into this world, not to condemn but to heal, to bring life overflowing, the fullness of joy. Set our hearts on our Savior; direct our wills to follow him as we humbly obey your righteous commands. In the blessed name of your Son, our Lord Jesus Christ, and in the fellowship of the Holy Spirit, amen.